LISTEN, PROPHETS!!

by

George A. Maloney, S.J.

DIMENSION BOOKS

Denville, New Jersey

Published by Dimension Books, Inc.
Denville, New Jersey 07834

To Reverend Bob Pate, Jane, Sister Joyce
and the Living Word of God Community
of Charleston, West Virginia

TABLE OF CONTENTS

INTRODUCTION

Jesus Christ is *the* Prophet who gives ultimate meaning to all other prophets. If a prophet in the Old and New Testament understanding of *Nabi* is one who stands in the place of God for the rest of his contemporaries, mediating God's word of salvific revelation to mankind, how perfectly must Jesus Christ, the *Word* of God enfleshed, be the perfect Prophet.

Jesus is the unique prophet because in His case the messenger is the message. Other prophets are "major" or "minor" to the degree that they have surrendered themselves to God as intermediates of God's message. But in Jesus Christ there is perfect correlationship between His Person and His prophet word. His Person was not a medium extrinsic to His preached word. His Person was the living Word manifesting immediately to those who believed in His word the Heavenly Father. His word would make men free (Jn. 8:32). Jesus Christ is the prophet par excellence because He is "inside" the word, effecting and actuating what the word stands for.

Above all, He is *the* Prophet because He gives man an immediate and absolute communication with God that leads eschatologically to man's ultimate salvation. He is the *Alpha*, the beginning of God's unified process of creation, redemption and sanctification. He is also the *Omega*, the goal or complete fulfillment of every human being, created "according to the Image and Likeness of God" (Gen. 1:26) that is Jesus Christ. "This is life eternal that they might know Thee, the only true God, and Jesus Christ whom Thou hast sent" (Jn. 17:3).

The true prophet in the Christian understanding, therefore, is one who is related to the Word Incarnate of God. He exists as a prophet to bring God's revealed word to men. He is an instrument of God's communication with men. He is not one who tells the future as such. Yet he is concerned to speak God's revealed message to men that necessarily is rooted in the future. For all of God's communications with man are aimed eventually in a linear progression into the future at leading man into God's eternal life.

In the Old Testament we find how the prophets were singled out by God to be possessed entirely by His message of salvation. Often like Jeremiah, they protested their inability. Yet God became their strength as they yielded to His word speaking in and through them. Their lives changed as God's messages formed the messengers into instruments of perfect docility and obedience to Him.

Amos preached a message of God's vengeance and death upon those who turned away from the Lord and a message of hope of new life for those who sought God. "Seek Me and live. . .Seek the Lord and you shall live" (Amos 5:4–6). Because he lived the message his message was effective.

Each prophet builds upon the preceding prophet and his messages. It is all one God speaking progressively and unfolding gradually a small corner of the mystery of His nature and of His eternal plan of salvation for mankind.

Isaiah taught the absolute holiness of God because he had been swept up by his experience before the awesome throne of God. There he heard the heavenly choirs of angels singing, "Holy, holy, holy is the Lord of Hosts. The whole earth is full of His glory" (Is. 6:3). He was a changed man. "For my eyes have seen the King, the Lord of hosts" (Is. 6:5).

God's holiness demands that Isaiah and the people to whom he was sent to preach God's message must live lives totally committed to God. God will intervene from His holy mountain when He wishes to save His people. Israel must respond to God's fidelity by faith and a total surrender to Yahweh.

The prophet is an intermediary for his people before God. He is a "servant" (Is. 20:3), serving the Lord to render God's message clear to His people. Above all, in *Jeremiah* and *Second Isaiah* on the eve of the Exile do we find the prophets not only becoming the suffering servants for their people in witnessing to God's word, but their message is prophetic in a more far-reaching way of pointing out in more complete detail the lineaments of the Suffering Servant of Yahweh, Jesus Christ.

Jeremiah announces the end of the Covenant of Sinai with its stress on external observation of the Decalogue and the laws of purification and declares the beginning of a New Covenant. This would build up the People of God by individuals being interiorly converted to God in their "heart." This Covenant would be confirmed by the suffering servant's total obedience to God. To know the will of God the servant had to speak interiorly and intimately with God. In that intimacy of hearts he would gain the strength to live in isolation. He cannot stop in his journey under God's hand. Yet he has complete trust in God.

> And they shall fight against thee, but they shall not
>   prevail against thee.
> For I am with thee to save thee and to deliver thee,
>   says the Lord.
> And I will deliver thee out of the hand of the
>   wicked and I will redeem thee out of the hand
>   of the terrible (Jer. 15:20–21).

In God alone, his guide, he finds his strength. "Blessed is the man who trusts in Yahweh, whose hope is Yahweh" (Jer. 17:7).

The prophet portrays the *new man*, the future of mankind, one who is turned totally within to Yahweh, his strength. He shows the world how to respond to the word of Love which, in the apt phrase of Jean de Yepes, is uttered in silence and eternally.

Jesus Christ comes as the fulfillment of this *new man*. In a most real way He teaches men how to be quiet to hear the Father's word. He lives His teaching in His prayerful relationship to His Father at Nazareth, in the desert and on the mountain top. He fasts. He weeps. He thirsts to bring all men to His Father's glory. He discerns His Father's will. "Not My will, but Thine be done" (Lk. 22:42). He prays. He hopes. He abandons Himself to His loving Father. He mediates His Father for the world. He dies. He is transfigured in glory.

He brings this world into its fullness. A new creation issues forth:

> The sun shall be no more thy light by day.
>   Neither for brightness shall the moon give
>   light unto thee.
> But the Lord shall be unto thee an everlasting light
>   And thy God thy glory.
> The sun shall no more go down.
>   Neither shall thy moon withdraw itself.

For the Lord shall be thine everlasting light.
  And the days of thy mourning shall be ended.
Thy people also shall be all righteous.
  They shall inherit the land for ever,
the branch of my planting,
    the work of my hands, that I may be glorified.
  (Is. 60:19–21).

But the transfigured universe would come about only by the Suffering Servant dying on the Cross. "And I, if I be lifted up from the earth, will draw all men unto Me" (Jn. 12:32).

The prophets of the Old Testament prepared for the coming of the Mediator and Prophet, King and High Priest, Jesus Christ. They exhorted the People of God, the *Anawim*, that small remnant of meek and humble, poor in spirit, merciful and peace-loving, pure of heart who lived in the desert and in exile waiting expectantly by total surrender to God for the coming of the Kingdom of God.

This, therefore, is not a book about the prophets of old. It is not concerned with the limits of the technical term of prophetism as found in the Old Testament. It is rather a message to the People of God of the New Covenant. *Listen, Prophets* acknowledges that Jesus Christ has called all of His Christian followers to be prophets in a broad application of the term. The concept of prophet is used as a model around which we can present teachings of the spiritual life that are as important today as they were in the days of the Old Testament prophets.

Each Christian, as the Decree on the Apostolate of the Laity of Vatican II points out, is made a sharer in the priestly, *prophetic* and royal office of Christ. He is called within the framework of his state of life, within his consciousness of being a living member of the Body of

Christ, by faith, hope and love which the Holy Spirit pours out into his heart, to promote the glory of God through the coming of His Kingdom and to obtain eternal life for all men. He is called to be a prophet by collaborating with the Word of God in mediating that saving, healing Word to others in the context of his daily life's activities.

Listen, Prophets is a call, an invitation to pursue the depth of this mysterious vocation buried within every true born-again believer. It is a guide to help everyone hungering for a deeper life in Christ Jesus, to find the reality of his vocation in ministering the Word of God to the people near him, whether he be a minister, counselor, mother, father, theologian or teen-age student. All are to waken to the Word living within them. "Today if you will hear His voice, harden not your heart. . ." (Ps. 95:7−8).

You are called to be *PROPHET*! You are not called to foretell the future events of history. But you are called by Jesus Christ to inspire, to edify, to lead others to the God of love by your very presence. By surrendering completely to His Word, your every word, gesture, action will mediate this divine presence to those around you.

God is calling forth a new people, a new body of believers to be His prophets in today's chaotic world. Such prophets are coming from every walk of life so that the Spirit of the Gospel will permeate and transfigure all into Christ. You and I are to be the prophets that Christ spoke of when He cried out: "Out of his belly shall flow rivers of living water" (Jn. 7:38). By moving under the power of Jesus' Holy Spirit our lives and good works will be a light drawing others to see the Word of God. "Let your light so shine before men, that they may see your good works and glorify your Father who is in Heaven" (Matt. 5:16).

Mother Teresa of Calcutta said that one drop changes the whole ocean and one person can change all mankind. May this book be a drop of water awakening in the hearts of all Spirit-filled believers the awareness of their prophetic vocation and bring it to fruition every moment of their waking day.

1

The Prophet Emerges

"Blessed is the man that hears me, watching daily at my gates, waiting at the posts of my doors" (Prov. 8:34).

The strange paradox in becoming a prophet of God is that to emerge as a prophet means to run away and be alone with God. The moment of emerging is reached when the prophet "demerges" himself. The butterfly emerges from the cocoon only to the degree that the caterpillar has turned into a chrysalis, detaching itself from all its former way of existence to be transformed into a new life. The prophet rises on fire with God, consumed by His burning love only when he has learned to turn aside from himself and stand stripped before the Almighty Burning Bush!

Moses in the desert, tending Jethro's flocks, heard God's command to take off his shoes. When he did, a new revelation of God came over him. God revealed Himself to Moses as a burning, devouring fire. But his first impulse was one of curiosity. He wanted to advance courageously to see this strange spectacle. He is ready to question God. He wants to comprehend by his own powers, to know the exterior "why" of God through his rational considerations. The first thing in the emergence of Moses as a prophet is not to emerge as he was, but to put off that part of the old Moses. God creates a prophet as a "new creation." The first step, therefore, in the emergence of a prophet to go forth to liberate God's Chosen People from the slavery of sin is that the prophet must meet God in mystery.

> And the angel of the Lord appeared unto him in a flame of fire out of the midst of a bush. And he looked and, behold, the bush burned with fire and the bush was not consumed. And Moses said, 'I will now turn aside and see this great sight, why the bush is not burnt! And when the Lord saw that he turned aside to see, God called unto him out of the midst of the bush and said: 'Moses, Moses.' And he said, 'Here am I.' And He said, 'Draw not nigh hither. Put off thy shoes from off thy feet for the place whereon thou standest is holy ground. Moreover I am the God of thy father, the God of Abraham, the God of Isaac and the God of Jacob.' And Moses hid his face for he was afraid to look upon God (Exod. 3:2–6).

God must take the initiative to call the prophet. He freely chooses His servant but the one condition that He demands is that the future prophet takes off his shoes, loses all of his securities and protections. He must strip himself of all his own ideas that he has of God. God is holy, incomprehensible, ungraspable by human power. He is inexplicable. Nietzsche once said: "A thing explained ceases to interest us; this is why God will always interest us."

The prophet must be ready to meet God in faith and not in a clear vision. St. Paul had said: "For now we see through a glass, darkly; but then face to face. Now I know in part; but then shall I know even as also I am known" (1 Cor. 13:12). The moment of the emergence of the prophet is not when he advances towards God under his own power but paradoxically when he falls back in humility before the transcendent God. God is not a land to be conquered by man's force, but a Holy Land to which the prophet approaches with bare feet, a symbol of total emptiness of his power.

When the prophet is ready to accept no longer to have his pre-conceived ideas about God, God will then reveal Himself. How powerfully this is brought out in the scene of Moses before the burning bush. He experiences God as fire. He cannot seize the fire with his hands; he cannot hold God in his hands. Yet God reveals Himself to Moses as fire. This fire illumines and transforms Moses into God's prophet.

This process of illumination and transformation starts with the prophet holding himself poor and nude before the Ardent and Incandescent Bush. He says nothing for what can he say before the Ineffable? What thought can he think worthy of Him who is the Incomprehensible? In adoration he offers himself to this devouring Fire to be purified of all that is of independent self. God wishes to devour man. A prophet is therefore a man devoured by God! He forms one being with Him. He merges as iron merges into fire to become fire. He becomes "light from Light." He becomes divinized by God's very own life, transfiguring him into a true son of God. He participates truly in the very nature of God (2 Pet. 1:4).

This process of emptying in order that God may fill the prophet with His living Word is beautifully described by Charles Peguy in his poetical work, *Eve*:

> You know that God alone gives of Himself,
> And that man's being unceasingly decreases...
> And that God's being unceasingly goes back
> To its eternal source and its deep night
> And of itself produces its own growth
> And man's salvation and the world's strength.

There is a "breaking" process that is necessary, a process of putting off the sandals of our own control over life and ideas about God, ourselves and others.

EXODUS

It is a true exodus experience that is at the heart of every prophet as he emerges forth from a stage of lesser being to be led by God into darkness, the desert of his own poverty and nothingness, and there the wild God of Mt. Sinai will have His way to reveal Himself as He is, when He wishes, to whomever He wishes. He will then speak to the prophet who has "passed over" from his false self into a being, hungry and thirsty to receive the Word of God as the parched desert earth opens itself to the soft dew that covers it and stirs the seeds lying dormant into new and beautiful life.

The prophet in this process is undergoing a dying experience in an effort to "let go" and surrender himself totally to the transforming power of the Word of God. Moses learned at the burning bush to let go in order to hear God's revelation of Himself. By emptying himself he was in a new position to experience God's revelation as being Yahweh, "I am who am!" This was no longer a concept about God for Moses. God was now He who *is* in his life!

Moses thus was able also to speak God's Word to the Israelites in Egypt and stir in them a similar desire to "let go," to pass over from the flesh pots of slavery on to a new level of existing as God's people. They passed over the Red Sea, a form of their spiritual baptism under the power of the Holy Spirit described in the Exodus story as the cloud that accompanied them as they passed over into the desert. St. Paul says: "And they were all baptized unto Moses in the cloud and in the sea" (1 Cor. 10:2). The cloud protects the prophet as he makes the exodus:

And the pillar of the cloud went from before their face and stood behind them. And it came between the camp of the Egyptians and the camp of Israel. And it was a cloud and darkness to them, but it gave light by night to these, so that one came not near the other all the night (Exod. 14:19–20).

The prophet moves under the cloud of the Holy Spirit farther into the desert. It becomes more arid, darker, more frightening. Man wants to touch God, hold Him, control Him. He looks back toward the days of Egypt where there was security at least, even though it was enslavement. He is faced with a crisis as the Israelites were as they complained to Moses:

What shall we drink?. . .Would to God we had died by the hand of the Lord in the land of Egypt when we sat by the flesh pots and when we did eat bread to the full. For you have brought us forth into this wilderness to kill this whole assembly with hunger (Exod. 15:24; 16:3).

Only when the prophet experiences such a thirst and hunger to cry out to God to satisfy his longing will God become his food and drink, give him sweet water and Heavenly Manna. Yahweh will show mercy to His emerging prophet when he is broken and will allow God to have His total way with him. With St. John the Baptist in the desert, the prophet can shout out to God: "You must increase; I must decrease!"

The formation of the prophet like the butterfly in the cocoon takes place in the darkness of emptiness where God's presence is more felt as an absence, where knowledge of Him seems to be total ignorance. Then the prophet is ready to emerge because he is ready to let God speak His Word at any time, in any place, with any accent. God's Word will come through the prophet clearly towards His

People because the prophet in his poverty and utter emptiness has allowed God to speak His Word without any static or disturbance from himself.

IT IS GOD WHO SPEAKS

The other part of the emerging prophet is that once he has been hollowed out by God's purification of all that is sheerly of man, then God speaks and communicates Himself, no longer in concepts and words, but in the Gift of His Word. "Be still and know that I am God" (Ps. 46:10). The amazing experience of the emerging prophet is that God is always communicating His Word. It is only when he interrupts it with a self-assertion that communication is broken.

This communication is similar to our experience of human love. When we understand that God is not this way in His communication because He follows our experience of human communication in deep, personal love but solely, because God is this way, thus human beings, made according to His image and likeness, also communicate. Or put in a truer fashion, human beings communicate in a manner similar to God because in true human love it is God who thus communicates Himself to us in the very experience of human love.

Man moves about this earth as Adam in the Garden of Eden. God had given him all the wonders of myriads of creatures and he was to cultivate them, order and bring them into a harmony. But man was lonely. "But for Adam there was not found a helpmate for him" (Gen. 2:20). God gave him Eve, a human being, an equal who could look at him with a look, a smile, who could speak a word that would dissolve his solitude. God had made him for such an encounter that through a smile or a look or a touch or a word he could enter into a relation of love, of self-giving. We know that we exist suddenly in a new way because we have been recognized by name and loved by another.

Mary the Virgin Mother was overwhelmed with joy in seeing herself loved by God. The prophet in solitude and quiet turns to God and experiences His love. But the amazing thing is that God never begins to love us. He does not begin to love because we have done something to first love Him. God has first loved us and we were brought into existence by His free love.

The prophet does not go into the desert to search for God but he goes there to discover that it was God all the time standing at the door of his heart (Rev. 3:20), knocking for admittance. Julian Green in his *Journal* writes: "God is dying of coldness. He knocks on all the doors, but whoever opens? The room is taken. By whom? By ourselves."

The prophet in the desert discovers that he himself is the main obstacle preventing God from transforming him into His prophet. So he undergoes the dying process, the emptying out of his heart so that God who has been waiting to enter may come and fill him up with His very own Being. And in that emptiness God speaks His Word.

His Word that He speaks expresses His entire being. St. Paul describes God's Word, Jesus Christ, as the perfect image of the invisible God (Col. 1:15). How often when a person speaks a simple word we see in that word the gift of that person. He wishes to communicate himself freely, giving himself completely to us. Likewise with God. His Word expresses an infinite love which He brings to us. "God so loved the world that He gave His only begotten Son, that whoever believes in Him should not perish but have everlasting life" (Jn. 3:16). God speaks His Word and through the Word He says: "I love you."

At times the desert so reveals to man his nakedness before God's great love that he is tempted to disbelieve God's goodness and love for him. To pray is to remain in the embrace of the Father, moved by compassion at the sight of the misery of the Prodigal Son (Lk. 15:20). God's love becomes greater the more we realize our sinfulness. The prophet remains in silent adoration with only one thought: "Me He loves; God loves me!" Nothing burns out our coarseness and selfishness more than to approach the Burning Bush and experience God's ardent love for us. The prophet emerges out of this amazement that the Trinity, Father, Son and Holy Spirit love him.

GOD'S INTIMATE PRESENCE

If Moses typifies the prophet who has met God in His awesome transcendence, then Elias shows us the emerging prophet who is wrapt up in intimate communion with a tender, loving God. On Mount Sinai in a theophany of terrifying thunder and lightening, God manifested to Moses His awesome holiness. Elias is one who hears God intimately present as a still, delicate voice from within.

Elias stands before God ready to serve Him. He had already spoken the word of God before Ahab. He had an apostolic heart to serve the Lord only. But his response is to say: "As the Lord God of Israel lives, before whom I stand. . ." (1 Kgs. 17:1). The prophet burns with zeal to serve God. Yet God first has to teach him that He has no need of his services. The first and most important service of the future prophet is attention and presence. God wishes the prophet to stand before Him. God offers to share His delights with him (Prov. 8:31). The emerging prophet must drown himself in the intimate, loving presence of the Lord. To pray is to lose freely one's time, one's whole being before God. It is a grace of being joyous with Him and of perceiving more and more His loving, abiding presence.

Before the prophet can reach this sense of intimate presence, like Elias, he must be led by God into the desert, into solitude, into an emptying, even to the point of discouragement. St. James says: "Elias was only a man submitted to the same miseries as we" (Jam. 5:17). But at the end of the 40 day journey through the desert, Elias deeply experiences the intimacy of God. The prophet, like Moses, needs to experience God as the Most High. But he must also come close to God as Elias did and feel the breath of God as a soothing breeze upon his tired face that revives his weakened spirit.

When God speaks His Word as a gentle whisper from within the psalmist gives us our response: "Your word is joy to my heart" (Ps. 119:111). Such a joy comes from discovering that God is the most tender Lover of man and is not outside us but "in Him we live and move and have our being" (Acts 17:28). The revelation that Elias teaches the emerging prophet is an experience of God's intimacy which is revealed to the purified prophet in a paradoxical manner that only experience can render possible because, once it has been experienced, no matter how paradoxical it remains to our human way of reasoning, the actual experience convinces us of its reality.

When God creates us, He is not "another" standing outside of us like some other object, different from ourselves. Yet we are not God; we are different from Him. How can God be different from us and still not be "another" standing outside of us? Elias learned this through the experience he had of the intimacy of God in all His gentle, delicate, loving presence to him on top of Mount Horeb. At the source of such a revelation of God is the experience in prayer that the prophet has of God looking at him and in that look of love He *is* continually creating the prophet according to His Word. God is constantly "calling" the prophet into being. He looks fondly with love upon him and as man yields to this "still, small voice" he becomes the being God wishes him to be. R. Guardini well describes this in his book, *Living God*:

> God turns His face to man and thereby gives Himself to man. By looking at me He enables me to be myself. The soul lives on the loving gaze of God: this is an infinitely deep and blessed mystery. God is He who sees with the eyes of love, by whose seeing things are enabled to be themselves, by whose seeing I am enabled to be myself.

This creative, loving presence of God within man inserts itself into him as a universal, constant presence of love. *Psalm 139* brings this creative presence of God into us in the most intimate manner. We exist out of the infinite love of God for us.

Elias teaches the modern prophet that to pray is to render consciously this existential dialogue between God and himself which extends itself then in a thrust outwardly toward others. God calls each of us by our name (Is. 43:1). He is the source of our liberty to surrender ourselves to His creative power in order to be the person He wishes us to be. Prayer is experiencing this intimate, creative presence of God within us, calling us into more complete being by inviting us to surrender ourselves totally to His creative love within us.

How often in the Bible, especially the Psalms, God is given human attributes or attitudes. God leans toward man, He sees, knows, hears, listens, understands, is near, receives, has pity on man. But all of this is to say that God wishes to enter into communion with man. God's nature is Love and the essence of love is to share. What better way to express what Elias experienced on the mountain top than to say that God is a mother? It is interesting to note that in Hebrew the word used to express the love which God has proved for us is *Rabamim*, which is the plural of "maternal womb." God's love that Elias experienced and all emerging prophets must experience on the desert mountain top is the love of a mother, multiplied to infinity. He is a father, a spouse, a friend, but all the love relationships suggested by such images pale before the experience of God, the Father, Son and Holy Spirit, living and loving within man.

God in prayer turns the one He is calling to be His prophetic servant and looks at him with love. In that look the prophet sees his proper face, his real self. The look of a man is the open door into the depths of his heart. It is in the look of our loved ones that we discover ourselves and are loved by them. How much more true this is of God. He looks but His gaze is one of perfect love, infinite tenderness, the closest intimacy. God looks at us with all the possibilities that He is calling us to and invites us to accept His call. He sees our sins and potential for future evil for nothing can be hidden from Him. Yet the prophet has an overwhelming experience that God tenderly, intimately loves him.

True prayer that is the opening of the prophet's door to let God have complete dominance in his life is to penetrate into the look of God and desire to be seen

through and through by Him, even to the depths of the
most secret areas of his being. The prophet cries out in
prayer for that continual healing that can come only
through an experience of being loved by Love itself. To
desire to be healed is to be healed! To desire to look upon
the face of God is to see Him already. "Lord, make Your
face shine on us and we will be saved" (Ps. 80:4).

The prophet begins to live in the light of God's
countenance shining within him. Friendship is born; there
is the continued assurance of being loved by God in each
moment of life. "Thy watchmen shall lift up the voice;
with the voice together shall they sing, for they shall see
eye to eye" (Is. 52:8).

At the heart of the prayer of a Christian prophet is
the continued, healing, loving gaze of God. But this God is
a community, Three Persons sweeping the prophet and
through the prophet all men into a similar community of
love. Fr. M. D. Molinie, O.P. describes Christian prayer:
"The Christian contemplation is trinitarian, the fire of two
looks which are devoured by Love." At the heart of the
Trinity the Persons look at each other and give themselves
to each other in a mutual love. In Baptism Jesus Christ
sent us the Holy Spirit who makes it possible for us to
communicate with God's look of love.

It has been said that to love serves for nothing, but it
changes everything. When God encounters the prophet, a
covenant of love is established and the prophet emerges.
God says: "I am your God and you are My child. Here is
My eternity, My very own power and life, My sanctity.
Let's put it together with your daily, earthly life, with
your poverty, even your sinfulness, your many failures,
but also let's put it together with the potential I have
placed within you from all eternity to respond to My

Word. Your existence now is one of being united with My very being. Nothing can separate us for I am God and I am faithful always to my covenant."

The prophet like Elias can leave such a mountain experience of God's beauty and intimate love to serve the world because he knows that he is rooted in a community of God's love. Jesus Christ is God's Word that is being continually spoken in the prophet's heart. Before the prophet can go forth to speak God's Word, he needs yet other elements. It is one thing to experience God's intimacy. It is another thing to thirst for greater intimacy. The Prophet cannot live without God. His thirst pushes him forward to desire to be consumed in this divine love. St. John of the Cross describes the emerging prophet who thirsts for greater union with God:

> I live, yet no true life I know
> And living thus expectantly,
> I die because I do not die.
> Within myself no life I know
> And without God, I cannot live.

2

The Prophet Studies To Be Quiet

"Thou wilt keep him in perfect peace whose mind is stayed on Thee" (Isaias 26:3).

Perhaps the greatest need in our modern world is quiet. We are being torn into so many directions. Our nerves are taut and frayed. Tenseness shows itself not only in our cigarette chain-smoking and indigestion but above all in our inability to reach that still point of concentration on whatever task is at hand. There are many conferences, seminars and courses. Yet how few of them are devoted to the study of quiet? There can be no deep contact with God unless we can return to that quiet and silence which take us into God's holy presence. God before He ever began to create and speak His various words lived in silence. The Word that was with God in the beginning before time and creation issued forth from God in utter silence. God's simplicity was a quiet sigh of love that poured forth from Father into Son and from Son back to Father.

Man needs to break his fragmented world that is constantly being punctured by noises to enter into that primeval, endless *now* of God's quiet. Here he enters into a state of *being*. It is not passivity or lack of activity. It is beyond such descriptions. It is where life and love merge into the same experience.

This experience of silence and solitude is so necessary for today's world. There, is a great hunger for the Lord. "As the hart pants after the water brooks, so pants my soul after Thee, O God. My soul thirsted for God, for the living God; when shall I come and appear before God?" (Ps. 42:1–2). Everywhere one goes,one finds this hunger, this thirsting for a deeper walk with the Lord. Many people after they have received the Baptism of the Spirit soon tire of continual prayer meetings with endless singing. In their own personal lives there seems to be no growth. Christians must help one another to grow in an appreciation of silence and stillness ". . . in quietness and in confidence shall be your strength" (Is. 30:15).

It is only in returning to silence and stillness that the prophet will make genuine progress in his own spiritual growth as well as mediate this presence to others. This is truly the prophet's duty. He must STUDY TO BE QUIET. He needs time each day to be deeply immersed in the presence of the Lord in periods of quietness that will work great signs and wonders in his life towards others.

All are not called to become famous writers, preachers or politicians, but all Christians, regardless of their state in life, are called to mediate this presence by a certain quietness about their whole being.

We do not realize how accelerated our lives have become. Psalm 37 advises us: "Fret not thyself" (Ps. 37:1). Even religious, priests and ministers by profession do not realize how accelerated the pace of their own lives has become. What are we doing to our physical bodies by this fast living? Actually destroying them! And the same question can be asked of our minds. Anxieties and fears, hatreds and violence, suppressed inside of our minds, destroy all peace and eventually any joy and happiness that had been there before.

GOD SPEAKS GENTLY

Why are there so few contemplatives today, so few men and women of deep prayer? Why aren't there more prophets in today's world? The answer is that there are so few who are willing to study how to be quiet. Few of us are willing to step out of this accelerated rat-race of modern living with its overstimulation and super-excitement and live at God's rate. God gets things done and they are done right. He works without rush and noise. Even when He spoke to His Prophets in the Old Testament, we find Him speaking in the gentle breeze: "a still small voice" (1 Kgs. 19:12).

If we want to be prophets of silence, listeners of the Word, we must learn to carve out large segments of our busy day for silence and solitude. We must learn to go back to the quietness of the woods and forests. We must learn to draw upon the vast richness of solitude that the physical world has to offer us. That is why whoever recognizes his call to be a prophet must go back to the woods, seek the desert places, mountains and deserts as a retreat from this confused and broken world.

Recently I had an opportunity to spend three months on a farm, quite all alone, in Georgia. In the evening especially it was so refreshing and regenerating to sit by the lake and watch the sun go down upon the quiet waters. As night brought peace and rest to all of nature, frogs and unseen insects began their nightly chorus. In the early morning hope was vividly experienced in the flaming colors spangling the scattered clouds of the sky. The birds seemed to be shouting to the world to wake up and be alive and filled with hopeful joy. Such moments may be infrequent in our busy urban lives but Jesus Himself has invited us to "come apart and rest awhile" (Mk. 6:31). The prophet must discipline himself to quietness, to drink in the beauty of nature if he is to grow.

Corrie Tee Boom says that the whole world is a classroom and we can say that Mother Nature is the classroom for the future prophet. He must learn to experience the peace of God of which St. Paul speaks that "surpasses all understanding" (Phil. 4:7). It is only in peaceful quietness that the prophet will become consciously aware of God's presence. As he learns to walk with God, this coordinating peace of God will flow into his mind and heart and body. Yes, even his nerves and muscles will experience this healing effect of the Divine Healer's presence.

Our Oriental brothers and sisters are far ahead of the Westerners in this matter of peaceful composure of body and spirit. There, everything is geared to attain unity of body and mind. The wives arranging their bouquets of flowers in the morning put them according to a harmonious pattern that comes from within. Then the external flower arrangement helps to foster such harmony in anyone who gazes upon the flowers. Pregnant mothers are encouraged not to listen to anything that would disturb the peaceful rhythm of the child growing within them. The Japanese tea-ceremony is not so much a social affair as a time of prayer and reflection, an exercise in gaining an integration of body, soul and spirit. Those of us who have experienced such a ceremony will never forget the economy of movement, gesture, word. The prophet learns also the art of controlling the mind to foster mental quiet. It ultimately means the complete surrendering of ourselves to God's presence and power.

Once in a conference to a group of women, one remarked: "What you say is all good and nice. But how can a mother like myself find time to be quiet and alone? Go into a secret closet! I don't even have a place to put my vacuum cleaner let alone putting myself in also! Have a time for solitude! I tried that, too. But it doesn't work. For inevitably the phone rings or one of the kids comes in bleeding." But she kept trying and she did succeed. A friend of mine, a busy contractor with a family of six growing children, fills the bath tub each evening after work and there he has his solitude with God.

How is the modern prophet in his busy work-a-day world or the prophet-mother to achieve this state of quiet, peaceful, efficient living? Just as we take courses in every other field we want to master, so, too, it is never too late to learn how to be quiet. But where can the prophet go to learn this art so much needed of quietness and stillness?

Even the busiest man or woman will find the time if he earnestly seeks it. Once in speaking of prayer to a group of nuns who invited also their friends to attend the conference I had this brought out very forcefully by a woman who was quite amazed that after such a conference on prayer none of the nuns had any questions, seemingly reflecting very little interest in prayer. She said: "I teach with many of you sisters in the nearby grade school. I am also the mother of seven children. Besides that, my husband is an alcoholic. I have to get up an hour before I normally would to touch God each day or I would not have the strength to continue." Once one is convinced of the necessity of moments of quiet for deeper communion with God there will be found time in a busy day for such a priority.

Rev. David Wilkerson decided once to turn the TV off for a half-hour of quiet in the evening in order to find time to be alone with God. Think of the thousands of young people whose lives have been affected by his decision to turn to a period of quietness before the Lord!

We should get into the habit of stopping often during to day to "pull ourselves together" by confronting God deeply within us as the Ground of our being. We take time out hopefully for physical exercises and recreation and eating three meals a day along with adequate sleep. We should also give time and effort to keep the mind quiet and let peaceful thoughts dwell in the mind, centered in love upon the indwelling Trinity living within.

Riding along the highways to work and "feeling" the rhythm of the car on the road can put us into a peaceful harmony with God. Listening to raindrops falling gently on the roof as we seek sleep can be a great quieting force. Looking at a flower, a lighted candle in a darkened room, a crucifix, a picture of beauty, or even focusing our attention on the powerful, quieting harmony in uplifting music can all help us to reach that "still point" where God is met most powerfully and most clearly speaks to us His saving Word.

Silence and tranquillity are necessary if we are to hear the Word of God. It cuts through our human way of seeing things and divides it from God's vision of reality.

> For the Word of God is quick and powerful and sharper than any two-edged sword, piercing even to the dividing asunder of soul and spirit and of the joints and marrow and is a discerner of the thoughts and intents of the heart (Heb. 4:12).

It is truly entering into the "seventh day of rest" where

we are swept up into the calm of God Himself. "And God did rest the seventh day from all His works" (Heb. 4:4). This is the freedom of the children of God, free to do always what most pleases their Heavenly Father.

Without such quiet there can be no growth in deeper, prayerful union with God. Attentive listening to the Word of God is a dying process to that autonomous "managerial" hold we have on our lives and above all on God as we busily either forget Him or fashion images of Him that become static little idols before which we bow and do reverence. But the living God of Abraham, Isaac and Jacob waits for us in the desert of our silent selves to reveal Himself to us in His own time and in His own words.

The great Flemish mystic of the 14th century, Jan Ruysbroeck, speaks of this attentive listening to the Word of God. He wries in his *Mirror of Eternal Salvation:*

> Above the reason in the depths of the intelligence, the simple eye of the contemplative soul is always open. It contemplates and gazes at the light, the Word. With pure gaze, enlightened by the Light itself, eye against eye, mirror against mirror, image against image.

By learning to find time in a busy day to stop and do as the Psalmist says, "For unto Thee, O Lord, do I lift up my soul" (Ps. 86:4); the modern prophet silences his heart and in the quiet hears God speak. He becomes refreshed by that Word and he pours out that peace to all whom he meets. "Come unto me, all you that labor and are heavily ladened and I will give you rest" (Matt. 11:28).

The prophet's vocation is to proclaim Jesus, the Living Word, to the world. And what better way can we do this than by proclaiming Jesus through a life that has been stilled, quieted in moments of precious listening to that Word?

3

The Prophet Heals

"I am the Lord that heals thee" (Exod. 15:26).

When Jesus Christ appeared in Palestine among men, He, who was the perfect image of the Heavenly Father, acted out in human actions and words the inner life of His Father. The Synoptic Gospels are precisely a compilation of His preaching and healing ministry.

And Jesus went about all Galilee, teaching in their synagogues and preaching the gospel of the kingdom and *healing all* manner of disease among the people (Matt. 4:23; also Matt. 9:35).

We see Him filled with compassion at the physical, psychical and spiritual sicknesses that held His people in bondage. He came to announce the coming of God's Kingdom. Isaiah and Jeremiah had predicted the new times when tears would be wiped away and sorrow would be no more, because God was going to work a new thing among His people.

But when He saw the multitudes, He was moved with compassion on them, because they fainted and were scattered abroad, as sheep having no shepherd...And when He had called unto Him His twelve disciples, He gave them power against unclean spirits, to cast them out and to heal all manner of sickness and all manner of disease. (Matt. 9:36, 10:1).

35

Jesus came to give us forgiveness from our sins and total health of body, soul and spirit. He was the incarnation of Yahweh-*Rapha*, "I am the Lord that heals thee." Sin brought the death of God's life to our souls and diseases to our bodies. The Second Adam, Jesus, came to undo the work of Satan. He was made "sin for us" (2 Cor. 5:21). He "healed *all* that were sick that it mught be fulfilled which was spoken by Esaias the prophet, saying, Himself took our infirmities and bore our sicknesses" (Matt. 8:16-17).

Here we have an inspired commentary on a text of Holy Scripture by the Holy Spirit, assuring us that the words found in Isaiah 53:4; *choli* and *makob*, refer literally to our sicknesses and our pains. Dr. Young translates Isaiah's prophesy:

> Surely our sickness he has borne,
> And our pains he has carried them,
> and we — we have esteemed him plagued,
> Smitten of God and afflicted.

And in verse 5, Isaiah foretells that the Messiah would be bruised for our iniquities "and by his bruises there is *healing* for us."

Jesus spent His entire public life fulfilling this prophecy. He heals all who are brought to Him as a foretelling of what He still wants to do for His people. We moderns have so divided man into parts that when it comes to the question of man's salvation, we limit the redemptive power of Jesus Christ to the saving of our souls. He comes to save the *entire* man, to heal man on all levels of his existence so that the seeds planted in him "according to the Image and Likeness of God" (Gen. 1:26), may fructify into a fully alive human being. God creates for life, for abundant life and Jesus comes that we may have God's life fully. When we are sick physically or mentally or spiritually, plagued by sicknesses of the body, the mind or the spirit, we are not what God created us to be.

CHRIST BRINGS US FULL HEALTH

The bodily diseases such as cancer and heart ailments are most evident to all of us. Yet the nation's no. 1 health problem lies in the area of not mere bodily diseases but rather in the area of emotional and mental illnesses. About nine million Americans are suffering severely from such disease. As many hospital beds are filled by the mentally deranged as are occupied by all medical and surgical patients combined. One out of every twenty Americans will have a psychotic disturbance severe enough to confine him in a hospital for the insane. All of us suffer from untold, increasing stresses, anxieties that, even though they do not cripple us completely, still render us not fully healthy and functioning at our top capacity as God would have us do.

We must believe, therefore, that God is vitally concerned with the whole man and his complete health. God wishes to give him a share in His *life* which is a life totally removed from any crippling disease. The New Testament Greek word for salvation is *soteria*, from *sozo*, which translates the Semitic root, *hajjim*. This was the Old Testament word to describe fullness of happiness, joy and peace, total health, the result of living a full, good life under God's protections and within His holy will.

Salvation, both in the Old and the New Testament, therefore, implies a total saving and healing of man by the

Savior, Jesus Christ, who possesses the healing power to
restore man to the sonship of God and to make him grow
into the even fuller participation of God's eternal life. God
through Jesus Christ wants *all* men to enjoy such total
health. As Jesus showed compassion and mercy upon the
multitude of sick persons brought to Him and He healed
them, so He shows us the heart of the loving compassionate Father. For God in the Old Testament to show
compassion (*rachamin* in Hebrew) and in the New Testament (*eleemos* in Greek) means that He loves His people
more tenderly than a shepherd loves his sheep, a mother
her child, a bridegroom his bride. He is desirous of doing
all to remove pain and suffering from His children's lives
and replace that with exuberant, rich, happy health.

God so loved the world, you and me, that He gave us
His only begotten Son (Jn. 3:16). Above all, in dying, He
ransoms us from the powers of darkness. Satan and his
forces of evil have no power now over us children of God,
all because of what Christ Jesus has done for us.

> Therefore if any man be in Christ, he is a new creature; old
> things are passed away; behold, all things are become new.
> And all things are of God, who has reconciled us to Himself by
> Jesus Christ and has given to us the ministry of reconciliation
> (2 Cor. 5:17–18).

Faith convicts us through God's revealed words in
Holy Scripture that God in Jesus Christ wishes to forgive
and heal all of us our sins and diseases. Holy Scripture is
not concerned to give us a scientific treatise showing how
spiritual estrangement from God through self-centeredness
paves the way for psychical as well as bodily diseases. It
merely tells us that God wishes to heal all types of diseases
and to restore His children to perfect health of body, soul
and spirit.

God's revelation is clear that Jesus Christ continues to do what He did in the Gospel narratives: to heal all who come to Him. God's promise to His Chosen People of the Exodus story is still being made and fulfilled through Jesus Christ in our regard:

> And God said, If thou wilt diligently hearken to the voice of the Lord thy God and wilt do that which is right in His sight and wilt give ear to His commandments, and keep all His statutes, I will put none of these diseases upon thee, which I have brought upon the Egyptians; for I am the Lord that heals thee (Exod. 15:26).

CHRIST COMMISSIONS OTHERS TO HEAL

Jesus meant His ministry of teaching and healing to continue through His chosen Apostles and disciples. He promised His twelve before His death that they would do His works and even greater ones than He did. "He that believes in Me, the works that I do shall he do also and greater works than these shall he do; because I go unto My Father. And whatsoever you shall ask in My name, that will I do, that the Father may be glorified in the Son" (Jn. 14:12–13).

Before He ascended into Heaven to be our intercessor at the right hand of His Father, He gave His great commission to His Church:

> Go into all the world and preach the Gospel to every creature. He that believes and is baptized shall be saved. . .and these signs shall follow them that believe: In my name shall they cast out devils. . .they shall lay hands on the sick and they shall recover. . .And they went forth and preached everywhere, the Lord working with them and confirming the word with signs following (Mk. 16:15–18).

The *Acts of the Apostles* is a book of these wondrous "signs" wrought by Jesus Christ through His Holy Spirit working in His chosen disciples.

> And by the hands of the Apostles were many signs and wonders wrought among the people...Insomuch that they brought forth the sick into the streets and laid them on beds and couches that at least the shadow of Peter passing by might overshadow some of them. There came also a multitude out of the cities round about unto Jerusalem, bringing sick folks and them that were vexed with unclean spirits and they were healed *everyone* (Acts 5:12–16).

We note that *all* were healed. St. Paul on the island of Malta healed the father of Publius by laying hands on him and praying for him. "Others also who had diseases in the island came and were healed" (Acts 28:9). Above all, St. James insists with the early Christian believers that if anyone is sick, those of firm faith should be called in to pray over him and anoint him.

> Is any sick among you? Let him call for the elders of the Church, and let them pray over him, anointing him with oil in the name of the Lord. And the prayer of faith shall save the sick and the Lord shall raise him up; and if he have committed sins, they shall be forgiven him (James 5:14–15).

THE MODERN PROPHET BELIEVES IN HEALING

Jesus Christ still wishes to heal all the sick. Sickness and disease as such give God no glory. Yet Jesus limits His healing power as He does His resurrectional presence to the strength of faith of those who believe in Him. How staggering a thought that He ties His healing presence to our faith in Him! And yet even in His earthly life, He limited His healing power to those who received Him as

Savior, the One who healed. In His hometown, there were many sick, yet He could heal only a few because of their great disbelief (Mk. 5:2—5). He had preached the necessity of faith: "If thou canst believe all things are possible to him that believes" (Mk. 9:23).

The modern prophet is the Christian who believes completely and confesses to the world in word and deed that Jesus Christ is true God and true man. He is Lord and Master in his life. He believes that his Lord can do all things and from Holy Scripture he believes that He wishes to heal *all* men. He has turned his whole life over to Him to let Him minister His healing word through him. He first has repented and received Jesus' healing on all levels. He knows this healing is a process that must continuously go on if his heart is to be always one with that of his Master. He has one will and that is to seek the glory of God at all times. He has no power except in the divine life of the Vine, Jesus Christ, that courses through him, the branch (Jn. 15).

Above all, his faith, constantly renewed within him by the outpouring of the Holy Spirit, gives him the strength to pray without wavering. He has heard and acted on St. James' words:

> But let him ask in faith, nothing wavering. For he that wavers is like a wave of the sea driven with the wind and tossed. For let not that man think that he shall receive any thing of the Lord. A double minded man is unstable in all his ways (James 1:6—8).

He literally believes in a vision of God's almightly presence that goes beyond his five senses. That divine power is capable of doing all things, if he only does not waver in his faith. He has pondered the words of his Savior, Jesus:

> If you have faith and doubt not, you shall not only do this which is done to the fig tree, but also if you shall say unto this mountain, be thou removed and be thou cast into the sea, it shall be done. And all things, whatsoever you shall ask in prayer, believing, you shall receive (Matt. 21:21–22).

His faith is "the evidence of things not seen" (Heb. 11:1) but nonetheless of things real, of God's loving power to heal all forms of sicknesses beyond the limits assigned by the present state of scientific knowledge. He looks to his Savior to accomplish what he knows is His wish—to be "Yahweh who heals."

Above all, he has heard Jesus Christ solemnly tell him:

> ...and who shall not doubt in his heart, but shall believe that those things which he says shall come to pass, he shall have whatsoever he says. Therefore I say unto you: What things soever you desire, when you pray, believe that you receive them and you shall have them (Mk. 11:23–24).

It is not faith to believe in Jesus Christ's fidelity to fulfill His promises after we have "seen" with our own physical eyes the healing of a sick person. The prophet heals because he believes that Jesus Christ has already healed before there is any manifested sign of a healing. The reason for such a healer's confidence without sign is trust in God's fidelity to fulfill His promises. God is faithful and He will keep His word. Because by God's grace the prophet abides in Jesus Christ and obeys His word, he knows he can ask anything of the Father in the name of Jesus and it will be granted him (Jn. 15:16, Lk. 11:9–13).

God always heals. The prophet prays over the sick of this world, not "if it be Thy will" to heal the sick but with childlike confidence that God will always heal, after he has turned to the Holy Spirit to pray for discernment in order to "put on the mind of Christ." He knows healing is never on the physical level alone and so he leads the sick to share his faith vision of God's healing. It is a process that, once it starts with the inner healing of the sick person's weak faith and the converted heart is turned totally to the Lord, for it continues to affect all levels of the sick person's being. He teaches the sick person to claim the victory in Jesus' name and to ask no longer for this or that specific healing, but rather to believe that the Father who knows our hearts' desires will grant the healing.

The Church today is beginning to see the results when modern prophets surrender in their own lives to the healing power of Jesus Lord and to that degree are able to lead others also to surrender to that deeper faith that allows them to believe that God does will always to heal all who call upon the Father in the name of Jesus Christ. In the early Church Christianity spread so rapidly, not because of any fancy sermons or even involvement on the social level to change society with new, clever structures, but it spread because of the child-like faith of Christians who had turned their lives over to God and lived radically the Gospel through a living faith in the healing power of God.

And today Jesus Christ is sending His Holy Spirit mightily upon modern-day prophets who have that same child-like faith to believe that all things are possible to God. No one ever is converted to surrender himself totally over to Jesus Christ unless he first has encountered one who presents a lived, preached faith, seen in the life of the prophet who points out the inner "reality" of God's loving presence, His compassion, His power that is ready to answer the prayers of those who "believe on Him whom He has sent" (Jn. 6:29).

For such a modern prophet the age of miracles and healings is not over. Jesus Christ promised His followers that if they believed on His word, greater things even than He did they will do. At least the modern prophet is not surprised to do the things that Jesus Christ did: heal the blind, the deaf, the dumb, drive away demons, cure the paralytic, the epileptic, the leprous. For he knows that God is Yahweh who heals. God wants to heal. He looks only for prophets who have faith enough to believe in the healing word of God and to give that healing word to the multitudes.

4

The Prophet Weeps

"Let my eyes run down with tears night and day and let them
not cease for the virgin daughter of my people has broken with
a great breach with a very grievous blow" (Jer. 14, 17).

The prophet stands on the mountain top and looks
into the face of God. His eyes scan the horizon and
wherever they stop, he sees the beauty of God's face
reflected: in the fluffy, pure clouds, the pine trees cloaking
the mountain side with a covering of fresh green, the
rushing mountain torrents eagerly seeking the peaceful
reunion with the ocean, the birds that take wing and soar
toward their Heavenly Father who feeds them and gives
them cause to sing joyfully.

He praises God for His infinite beauty. He stretches
his hands out to touch, grasp, possess Him, but his hands
close as the Unpossessable escapes him. He cries from out
of the depths of his soul to possess Him. He cries tears of
joy before God's beauty. He weeps to see how far He is
still away from him.

The modern prophet like the Prophets of old knows
that the closer he approaches the beauties of God, the
more aware he is of the arid sterility within his own heart.
He sees the scattered, dried bones strewn over the haunting
memories of bitter joys of yesterday and of what could
have been. As he looks upon the mountain of God's

grandeur, he sees the valley of his own nothingness. He turns within and experiences in the tomb of his inner darkness the light of God's tender love bursting upon him, ever so softly and healingly and tears well up in his eyes.

"Oh, God, forgive me my many transgressions."

Have mercy upon me, O God, according to Thy
  loving kindness,
According unto the multitude of Thy tender mercies
  blot out my transgressions.
Wash me thoroughly from my iniquity and cleanse me
  from my sin. . .
Purge me with hyssop and I shall be clean; wash me and
  I shall be whiter than snow. . .
Hide Thy face from my sins and blot out all my
  iniquities.
Create in me a clean heart, O God, and renew a right
  spirit within me.
The sacrifices of God are a broken spirit; a broken
  and a contrite heart, O God, Thou wilt not despise.
    (Ps. 51:1–2; 7; 9–10; 17).

The prophet becomes more and more aware of the need for a continued healing deeply within him. He experiences, especially in moments of standing before God in utter quiet and openness to His Holy Spirit, his sinfulness. His whole being "groans in travail" seeing its fragmentation. He feels caught in a prison of darkness and yet he sees a delicate ray of light leading him out through the crack of *metanoia*, conversion unto the Lord. He hears the hopeful words of God whispered deeply within his soul:

Turn to Me with all your heart and with fasting and with weeping and with mourning. And rend your heart and not your garments and turn unto the Lord your garments and turn unto the Lord your God. For He is gracious and merciful, slow to anger and of great kindness and repents him of the evil (Joel 2:12–13).

Daily he experiences deeply within him what St. Paul so vividly experienced within his own being. Caught before the power of evil like an inner cancer gnawing at his vital organs, the prophet cries out for healing. He feels that inner principle or law warring within his members. He finds himself helplessly doing that which he knows he should not do.

I see another law in my members, warring against the law of my mind and bringing me into captivity to the law of sin which is in my members. O wretched man that I am! Who shall deliver me from the body of this death? I thank God through Jesus Christ our Lord (Rom. 7:23–24).

As the modern prophet sits within his inner desert like the Desert Fathers of old, he learns to yield himself to the indwelling presence of Jesus Christ, the only Divine Physician who can bring us life that we may have it more abundantly, God's very own life. He cries out with utter distrust in himself but with unbounded confidence and hope in Jesus the Healer: "Lord, Jesus Christ, Son of God, have mercy on me, a sinner."

He kneels in spirit as the prostitute did before Jesus at the dinner table of the Pharisee and pours out tears, washing His sacred feet.

'Her sins, which are many are forgiven; for she loved much. But to whom little is forgiven, the same loves little.' And He said unto her: 'Thy sins are forgiven...Thy faith has saved thee. Go in peace ' (Lk. 7:47–50).

As long as man continues to live unreflectively and superficially, he will not feel the need to cry out in tears and in a constant yearning for repentance. Jesus Christ hears the prayers and cries of the little ones, the "poor in spirit." For did He not Himself promise that "Blessed are those who mourn, for they shall be comforted"? Jesus Christ continually sends His Holy Spirit into the hearts of the humble and broken in spirit.

The Holy Spirit purifies the penitent soul and fills it with a new enlightenment. The prophet understands in a new way his relationship with God and himself and the world around him. Tears are like a new Baptism in the Holy Spirit. They make good the Master's words: "If anyone is not reborn of water and the Spirit, he cannot enter into the Kingdom of God" (Jn. 3, 5). The Spirit convicts the Christian of his unworthiness to be loved by God, to be a favored child of so loving a Father. The deeper is man's sorrow through the Spirit's illumination, the more the tears of compunction flow freely.

Like Job, the prophet cries out: "My friends scorn me; but my eye pours out tears unto God" (Job: 16,20). St. John Climacus gives us the common teaching of the desert prophets:

> Greater than Baptism itself is the fountain of tears after Baptism, even though it is somewhat audacious to say so. For Baptism is the washing away of evils that were in us before, but sins committed after Baptism are washed away by tears. We have defiled the Baptism received in infancy, but we cleanse it anew with tears. And if God in His love for mankind had not given us tears, few indeed and hard to find would be those in the state of grace.

The Holy Spirit fills the contrite of heart with a deep knowledge of God's tremendous love and mercy on the one hand and He convicts them, on the other, with a realization of their own poverty, sinfulness and unworthiness to stand even in God's presence. How often modern prophets enter into "the Baptism of the Holy Spirit" and have this experience of tears that flow profusely whenever they reflect upon God's goodness and their own ingratitude in the past.

The Holy Spirit's great work in the prophet's life is to open his mind and heart to the inner meaning of God's revealed words of Scripture. If the Spirit makes us to be born from above, on high, making us children of the Spirit, speaking to us deeply within our hearts and telling us that we really are God's children (Rom. 8:16), He also fills us with an abiding sense of sorrow for our sinfulness and ingratitude towards so great a loving Father.

TEARS FOR OTHERS

The prophet moves closer to God and is filled with a deep shame for being a prodigal son. In experiencing somewhat a reconciliation with the loving, forgiving Father, he remembers his brothers and sisters who still live far away from the Father's love, "eating the husks of swine" (Lk. 15:16). He cries day and night, like Moses, with outstretched hands: "Pardon, I beseech Thee, the iniquity of this people according unto the greatness of Thy mercy and as Thou hast forgiven this people from Egypt, even until now" (Num. 14:19).

Such a modern prophet knows that in many circumstances his charity toward his neighbor is exercised in his silent weeping over the hardness of his relatives, friends, countrymen, fellow human beings. He understands the anguish of the heart of Jesus looking over Jerusalem and weeping:

O Jerusalem, Jerusalem, thou that killest the prophets and
stonest them that are sent unto thee, how often would I have
gathered thy children together, even as a hen gathers her
chickens under her wings and you would not (Matt. 23:37).

As Jesus the Good Shepherd would go up into the
mountains to seek the one lost sheep, so the modern
prophet in praying, fasting and tears stands before God,
asking mercy for his fellow-man. "Let my eyes run down
with tears night and day and let them not cease for the
virgin daughter of my people has broken with a great
breach with a very grievous blow" (Jer. 14, 17).

How easy, unfortunately, it is today for the sincere
Christian to weep over the violence and hatred rife on our
streets, in our families, in our hearts. There is so much of
that everywhere. Materialism and eroticism, the cult of the
body along with the cult of Satan all turn the prophet
toward a God whose love has been spurned, whose
Kingdom has been replaced by the Kingdom of darkness.
With the Prophet Jeremiah, he too can wail for his people
who refuses to hear the Lord. "But if you will not hear it,
my soul shall weep in secret places for your pride and my
eye shall weep more and run down with tears because the
Lord's flock is carried away captive" (Jer. 13, 17).

EFFECTS OF TEARS

The prophet, therefore, seeks to remain in a state of
weeping before the Lord, begging pardon for his sins and
those of the rest of the human race. He finds as one of the
greatest effects of weeping for sins the extinguishing
within his heart of passions that formerly would burn him
with desires that would destroy the love of God in his soul.

The purified prophet puts to death any inordinate desires, reaching the stage of total submission to the will of God.

Thus so sensitized, the purified prophet can yield himself completely to the promptings of the Holy Spirit living within. Little static and opposition come from his sinful nature as he opens up in total submission to God's voice. "Speak Lord, Thy servant hears (1 Sam. 3:10). The hardness of heart yields through a repentant spirit to a docility of listening and a promptitude to do whatsoever God commands. Basically it is humility that reigns in such a purified soul, the humility of the Virgin Mary before God's wish that she serve Him as the Mother of the Savior. Only one who yields totally to the Holy Spirit as she did can respond: "Behold the handmaid of the Lord; be it done to me according to Thy word" (Lk. 1, 38).

But the greatest effect of the prophet's weeping is that the Holy Spirit fills him with "His fruit of love, peace and joy. ." (Gal. 5, 22). From the depths of his heart there flows out a radiating joy that even influences the body with a new-found health, happiness and cheerful countenance. And why should there not be felt such a joy? Did not Jesus promise to His disciples that they would be comforted after they mourned? (Matt. 5:4). He also promised in the Sermon on the Mount that others would persecute His followers, just as the prophets of old, but they should "rejoice and be glad, for a rich reward awaits you in Heaven" (Matt. 5:10).

An unruffled calm is given to the repentant prophet with an accompanied joy that no person or event can take from him. For Jesus Christ has conquered totally in his life. The purity of heart that allows him to see God in the sacrament of each moment fills him with happiness because all creatures proclaim the presence and love of

God for man. "At this sight you will grow radiant, your heart throbbing and full since the riches of the sea will flow to you, the wealth of the nations come to you" (Is. 60:3—4).

A strange alchemy exists between the sorrow for sins and the joy that flows from the realized experience of being transfigured into Jesus Christ. It is the Holy Spirit that quickens the prophet to a deep realization of what it means to be divinized by the Spirit of Love. It is joy, that joy that Jesus Christ, the greatest of the Prophets who learned how to weep for the sins of the world and to beg forgiveness of the Father for the ignorance of mankind, experienced on the Cross as He sought to do always what most pleased His Heavenly Father in spite of the agonizing suffering and death on Calvary.

In the Franciscan church of San Damiano in Assisi, there is a beautifully carved crucifix which, like most popular and ancient pieces of religious veneration, had a legend about how it was made. The story tells of a pious Franciscan Brother who started to carve out of a piece of wood a crucifix to honor the suffering Savior. After the corpus was finished, he became very perplexed as how to depict the suffering face of Jesus. He turned to the Lord in prayer but soon fell asleep. When he awoke, he found the crucifix finished, no doubt by the hands of an angel.

What is unique about this crucifix is the combined expressions on the carved face of Jesus. When one looks up at the crucifix from his right he sees tightly drawn lines showing a man in the throes of tremendous suffering. The left eye is taut and fixed in a stare of empty agony. But when one moves full center, he sees the lines elongated somewhat, giving the over-all impression of a man dying in great peace. But moving to one's left, he sees the lines artistically lengthened, a curl of a smile on the side of the lips, in general a picture of radiant, youthful joy.

The modern prophet knows that the transfiguration into Jesus Christ comes through a dying process. It is the Holy Spirit that purifies us by enlightening us to experience our sinfulness and how much darkness dwells within us, how much sickness and alienation there are still to be healed by the merciful love of Jesus the Savior. That same Holy Spirit gives us a second Baptism unto water, but this time the water comes from our interior weeping through an abiding sense of sorrow and shame before the awesome, loving God-Father. Weeping cleanses us from passions and attachments to ourselves as the center of our existence. It allows us in great, burning desire to live only for God. Joy is the paradoxical result of the prophet weeping. As he stands day and night in intercessory prayer for the salvation of the world through Jesus Christ, his sorrow turns to joy through the unshakeable hope that the Spirit breathes into him constantly. He looks up and sees the vision of the Lamb of God already in His glory. His weeping truly leads to joy and is turned into joy:

> . . .the throne of God and of the Lamb shall be in it.
> And His servants shall serve Him.
> And they shall see His face;
> and His name shall be in their foreheads.
> And there shall be no night there.
> They will need no candle,
> neither light of the sun.
> For the Lord God gives them light.
> And they shall reign forever and ever (Rev. 22:3–5).

5

The Prophet Fasts

"This kind goes not out but by prayer and fasting" (Matt. 17:21).

The modern prophet is God's fighter. He is sensitized to the gentle presence of God and in contrast he pains to see the shadows of the darkness of evil rising within the depths of his own being and that of the whole world, mounting like storm clouds to extinguish the last ray of light in the living world. Instead of retreat before the attack of evil in the world today, he knows from the Gospel teaching and the history of Christian Saints that the Kingdom of God is taken by force and violence (Matt. 11:12). Mahatma Gandhi, that great modern prophet, calls us back to the Gospel teaching when he said: "My religion teaches me that before a distress that no one can relieve, one ought to fast and pray."

Jesus Christ calls all of us to become modern prophets who face the forces of evil and by prayer and fasting command them to be driven out in His sacred name. "This type can be driven out only by prayer and fasting" (Mk. 9:29; Matt. 17:21).

PRIMITIVE MAN FASTED

A prophet is a total being saturated by the wisdom and knowledge of the Holy Spirit to know what makes man to be an integrated and whole person. When man strips himself of all pseudo-sophistication and returns, as the Gospel enjoins, to become like a little child in order to enter into the Kingdom of Heaven, i.e. into the basic relationships with the Almighty, Transcendent Being, God, he finds himself returning to fasting as an ethical and religious act necessary for a healthy total existence. Primitive man was aware of the ethical strength that could bolster the moral fiber of an individual or a community when he restrained his basic appetite for food.

More importantly man universally throughout all cultures and civilizations feels the need to fast in order to offer to God penance and propitiation for sins. Carl Jung speaks to the modern world of the universal need of all men in society to establish a *rite de sortie*, a way of providing a religious catharsis and thus a return of man and society once again to a new beginning and a new relationship with the Absolute.

Such fasting is an intentional abstention from food for religious motives. It is essentially an act of the higher nature of man, a prelude to a higher life of the spirit wherein he makes contact with the Unapproachable God. When man fails to control the amount of food he eats and freely indulges without any moderation, this disturbs the inner order of the spirit of dependence upon the Almighty.

The modern prophet comes to realize more than ever that he lives in an overfed society, whose members are literally eating themselves to death. What is he to do with such influence coming from a morally decadent society? He goes back to the Word of God to learn the secret of the early prophets, God's athletes, whose lives changed the lives of millions and made possible the impossible with God's grace.

THE PROPHETS OF OLD FASTED

It was through fasting that the Israelite nation was able to get a new grip on the God they sought, overcame all obstacles and received communication from God that led them into the Promised Land. Daniel fasted for twenty-one days. Elijah the prophet fasted for forty days and nights until he heard the still small voice speaking to him. When all else failed, it was fasting that turned the tide. Prayer in the life of these ancient warriors changed things, but when fasting was added to prayer it had the greatest effect in obtaining God's mercy and assistance.

Moses was a great prophet. When he came down from the mountain, he was met with the greatest crisis of his life. It is true God had spoken to him from the burning bush and had commissioned him to lead his people out of Egypt. For forty years he lived the life of a shepherd, caring for the sheep of his father-in-law. Never had he dreamt of leaving them. But God had other plans for him.

The modern prophet, similar to Moses, must make a choice to accept the call of the Spirit or reject it. Man stands always at the crossroads, one leading to God and the other away from Him. The Spirit-filled Christian can find true happiness only in God. He needs the peace with God and fasting is still an important practice in the life of the prophet helping him to grow in a real sense of dependency and creatureliness toward God along with his own poverty and sinfulness. It is this very recognition of one's own sinfulness that calls down God's mercy and justice upon all mankind.

At the burning bush, God commissioned Moses to lead the children of Israel out of Egyptian bondage into the Promised Land. So too the modern prophet in his office or the worker on a building project through the busy work hours or the prophet mother in her kitchen is commissioned to lead those nearest to him or her out of the bondage of the evil one. So many are plagued by the bondage of hate, revenge, pride, envy, money. The modern prophet must lead, like Moses, "his brothers out of the bondage" of Satan. Just as the Israelites had turned from the true God who led them out of bondage, so has modern man turned his face away from God. God is still saying to the modern prophets:

> I have seen this people and behold, it is a stiffnecked people. Now therefore let Me alone that My wrath may wax strong against them and that I may consume them. And I will make of them a great nation (Exod. 32:9–10).

Moses, on coming down from his retreat on Mount Sinai, soon caught sight of the idols that the people had made for themselves and before which they bowed down in worship. Moses in a fit of anger broke the Ten Commandments and sent orders for the execution of the leaders of the rebellion.

In the greatest crisis of his life, what did Moses do? He returned to Mount Sinai, resolved not to eat until God undertook the situation for he knew that punishment for his people would follow unless he, a weak man, could prevail with God.

Prophets, are you listening? Do you recognize the situation of Moses as being very similar to that of today? God is calling you, His modern prophets. He is giving you a chance to fast in order to help save our world.

> And he was there with the Lord forty days and forty nights. He did neither eat bread nor drink water. And he wrote upon the tablets the words of the covenant the ten commandments (Exod. 34:28).

Moses really loved his brothers—his people. He was not a man of personal ambition, but rather he was seeking forgiveness for his people about to die under the judgment of God. In the agony of soul, he went to the Judge, the eternal God, and pleaded mercy for his people. He reminded God that if His people perished in the desert the heathens would say that God had brought them out of Egypt into the desert that He might consume them. "Turn from Thy fierce wrath and repent of this evil against Thy people" (Exod. 32:12). The prayer and fasting of Moses prevailed and God spared His people from extinction as a nation. Through fasting and continual supplication Moses saved his people from perishing. But even with that he was not satisfied. He wanted total forgiveness for his people.

> Yet now if Thou wilt forgive their sin; and if not, blot me, I pray Thee, out of Thy book which Thou hast written. And the Lord said unto Moses: 'Whosoever has sinned against Me, him will I blot out of My book' (Exod. 32:32–33).

And even then Moses was not satisfied. He entered into his third intercession. It was not enough that God had saved Israel as a nation from perishing. It was not enough that their names should remain in the book of life or that an angel should go before them into the Promised Land. Moses refused to go into the Promised Land, unless the very presence of God went also. So again, he continued with his prayer-fasting. And again God heard his prayer:

> My presence shall go before thee and I will give thee rest. And he said unto them: 'If Thy presence go not with me, carry us not up hence' (Exod. 33:14–15).

In the course of his fasting and supplication Moses had drawn very close to God. He even had the boldness to ask God for the privilege of witnessing His glory. And again his prayer was answered. God hid Moses in the cleft of the rock and let him behold a vision of His glory! And so the bridge that had been destroyed between God and His people was again rebuilt. The breach that could have spelled eternal doom for the Israelites had again been restored. Through fasting the broken communion with the Eternal God had been renewed. The forty days and nights on Mount Sinai in prayer and fasting had resulted in breaking the powers of darkness and moving the compassion of God.

Also in those days the Prophet Moses received all that he needed to fulfill him with the strength and vision he required for the days ahead in the dry wilderness to which he was called.

In the life of the Spirit-filled prophet of today, the Baptism of the Spirit is so important for a fast to derive its greatest advantage. The Spirit will lead His people to fast, not necessarily for forty days, but to a fast. There will be times in every Christian's life when the Spirit will lead him to fast, if he is ready to receive this invitation.

There are many issues in our lives wherein we must decide for or against the love of God. The spiritual life of every prophet is a battle, wherein he sustains many attacks from the enemy. The sources of these are many. They come from the pressures of his society, from his work, from his family, from his recreation. God has not called the modern man into a life of abjectness but unto freedom of His children. He does not expect His people to live in constant fear of sinning. Every temptation is not sin. To live, however, in constant fear of ordinary difficulties is not even human.

But God does permit temptations in our lives in order

to teach us the great lesson of the spiritual life: our complete dependence upon Him. Only in struggles, weaknesses and failures do we learn true humility. True growth in the spiritual life consists in learning that God is our Father and loves us dearly in all events of our lives. Once this truth has permeated our lives many of our troubles cease. No price is too great to pay for the possession of God. Fasting helps man to overcome temptations and live solely unto the Lord. The fasting that is truly recognized by God is that which is accompanied by humility, repentance and true sincerity of heart.

GOD'S FAST

Fasting must be fundamentally an act of offering oneself to God through the sacrifice of a humble and contrite heart. If fasting is a seeking therefore of God in true repentance and humility, the impulse must first come from God and not from our own power. Some people rush into a fast rather than wait for the moving of the Spirit. A friend illustrates this with his own experience. "I remember once I made up my mind to fast. The first morning I awoke with the worse headache I had had for ages. The next morning was a repeat performance. Then I realized I had not waited for the moving and timing of the Lord. After seeeking His counsel several days later, I was able to begin the fast and stick to it." So the prophet too must pray for the right moment and the right motive and the right kind of fast.

It must be the Holy Spirit who leads us into the deeper Christian values of fasting to prevent it from becoming a technique solely for health purposes or expanded consciousness or for whatever purpose that could so easily turn it into another idol. The Holy Spirit first enlightens us to see as we progress in the spiritual life how wounded and fragmented our human nature is. The inner principle that St. Paul speaks of in *Romans 7* that wars against us prevents us from arriving at moderation in all things and attaining that moderation sheerly by reasoning to it.

Fasting is not mere self-renunciation or self-discipline, arduously forged by the human will. It is an action that flows from a reflex consequence of experiencing what it means to live in Christ.

> That I may know Him and the power of His resurrection and the fellowship of His sufferings, being made conformable unto His death. If by any means I might attain the Resurrection of the dead. Not as though I had already attained it nor were already perfect; but I follow after, if that I may apprehend that for which also I am apprehended of Christ Jesus (Phil. 3:10–13).

The Spirit teaches us how to integrate the three levels of the body, soul and spirit into a "new man" in Christ Jesus. He teaches us to fast so that such an experience under His power will engender a state of balance and truthfulness that is called humility. This allows us to conduct ourselves properly towards God, our neighbor and the world according to God's mind.

It was this same Spirit that drove Jesus Christ into the desert to fast unto hunger for 40 days and nights. The modern prophet that is driven into the desert of his own barrenness to fast needs the Holy Spirit to give fasting its true significance as a religious, worshipful act, and it is He alone who can animate the fast so that it begins and ends as an act of religion. Fasting becomes such an act of adoration to God through the Holy Spirit. Like the

Prophetess Anna waiting in the Temple for the coming of the Lord, "worshipping with fasting" (Lk. 2:37) the modern prophet is led by the Holy Spirit to glorify God and allow Him to have complete control over his life. Like the Virgin Mary, he can experience what it means, humbled in one's poverty, to exalt the Lord.

> My soul magnifies the Lord and my spirit has rejoiced in God my Savior. For He has looked upon the lowliness of His handmaiden. . .He has filled the hungry with good things. . .Behold the handmaid of the Lord, be it done unto me according to Thy word (Lk. 1:46–48; 53; 38).

THE TEACHING OF JESUS ON FASTING

Jesus came to fulfill the Old Covenant. The same elements, inspired by the same Holy Spirit working within God's chosen people, as found in the Old Testament fasting were to continue in Christian fasting. Fasting was to be an appeal to sorrow for sins along with a propitiation for sins committed. It was an exercise of imploration to obtain God's mercy and protection. Daniel fasts to prepare to receive God's revelation (Dan. 9:3; 10:2). David fasts when he learns of the deaths of Saul and Jonathan or to obtain the healing of his son (2 Kgs. 1:12; 13:16; 21:23).

When Jesus began to teach about Christian fasting, He sought to correct the hypocrisy of the Pharisees who fasted externally without a true conversion of heart. Yet He wanted to give fasting a whole new dimension that it had not possessed in the Old Testament. There was to be no long faces during a fast; but joy would be the quality that would accompany the Christian fast.

> Moreover when you fast, be not, as the hypocrites, of a sad countenance; for they disfigure their faces, that they may appear unto men to fast. Verily I say unto you, they have their reward. But thou, when thou fastest, anoint thy head and wash thy face that thou appear not unto men to fast, but unto thy Father who is in secret. And thy Father who sees in secret shall reward thee openly (Matt. 6:16–18).

The joyful element that Jesus adds as a necessary ingredient to fasting does not take away from the suffering and dying process that is essential to a fast. But the Christian belief that Jesus "is risen and has trampled down death, granting death to those in the tomb" (prayer from Byzantine Easter Liturgy) fills the Christian faster with an experience of exultation and triumph even amidst the suffering and bite of a partial death, symbolized by fasting. Fasting leads to the spiritual surrender of self to God that gives the joy of the Holy Spirit (Gal. 5:22).

Fasting in the life of the modern prophet is an experiential living out of the eschatological hope central in the paschal mystery. While Christ was on earth, He was the bridegroom. He had come to establish the mystical marriage with God's People. How could His disciples fast and suffer during such a celebration of joy? (Matt. 9:14–15). The good news was at hand. The Kingdom of God was indeed close at hand in the very Person of Jesus Christ!

But after Jesus died and rose, His followers are found in a period of eschatological awaiting His full coming. "While we are in the body, we are *absent* from the Lord," says St. Paul (2 Cor. 5:6). The modern prophet waits in suffering, longing for the Bridegroom to return in all His beauty and glory. Yet this exile of suffering shows to the world a hopeful joy. This joy results from knowing that even now Jesus Christ has conquered in such a fasting experience the possession of our whole being. Even now we are "new creatures" raised to the sonship with Him, co-heirs forever of Heaven. Death can have no sting over us. This is what the prophet today announces chiefly to the despondent world. The suffering of this life, of this fasting, cannot be compared to the joys to come! Yet even now as he dies in such suffering, he experiences greater, unending, joyful union with the Lamb of God!

FASTING—AN ACT OF LOVE

Once the prophet through fasting has broken his independent hold over his life and surrendered himself totally into the loving hands of God, he finds a fresh openness in loving service towards others. He empathizes in a new consciousness with all the physical, psychical and spiritual needs of every human being. Walls of division and prejudices fall as he runs to meet the crying needs of his neighbor. He understands that he cannot take on all of the sufferings of the whole universe, of every broken man, woman and child. Yet fasting has given him a sense of his own poverty. He is the poorest of all God's children. When he learns of others suffering from a lack of food, clothing, housing, he cannot indulge any longer in any form of excess. He becomes a prophet not only of word but in deed! Here we see how actual, physical fasting develops the necessary spiritual fasting: controlled moderation in every area of sense, emotional and intellectual life so that all sinful thoughts, words and deeds are eliminated and universal charity reigns supreme. God has conquered in such a Christian's life and this is proved by his love for others.

God will raise up some modern prophets who will also be called not only to do penance for the immoderations of injustice of others but their fasting will be unto a "punishment" to the consciences of the guilty. Here we see how Mahatma Gandhi becomes the model for such modern prophets. He once said that he fasted as "a penitence for me and a punishment for all." For some modern prophets a fast should be public, demonstrated for all to see, a dramatic protest against certain abuses on the social or religious levels. For such "creative suffering" on behalf of others, to induce a change of heart in them, we can see what grave responsibility there is on the part of such prophets to move at each step in humble prayer under the power and guidance of the Holy Spirit.

Lanza del Vasto, one of Gandhi's disciples, wrote: "When you think of men starving in the world, you are forced to cry out for them with a more sensitive heart. One who fasts is made transparent. Others appear to him transparent. Their sufferings enter into him and he is without defense against them."

Today millions of people are suffering from hunger and drought; thousands are dying in such areas of the Sub-Sahara and in India and will continue to do so. True Christian love urges us to fast and make sacrifices to obtain God's mercy upon our unfortunate brethren and to touch the hearts of those most capable of coming to the help of such destitute people.

The Church will not impose in the future as it did in the past a minimal rule of obligation to fast and abstain from meat upon all Christians. But modern prophets will lead those in the deserts of our cities back to the power of fasting. They will show the lost and despondent through fasting and prayer how to hunger for God and then receive their fill. Fasting carves out of our hearts the loneliness that a surfeiting of this world's good has created and replaces it with a purity of heart that will allow us to see God. Not loneliness but aloneness, oneness with God will be the result.

As the Prophetess Anna in the Temple prepared by the Holy Spirit through prayer and fasting in solitude, so the modern prophet prepares himself and his people for the coming of the Messiah. She had become so sensitized by the Spirit in her waiting for the Lord through her fasting that, when Mary and Joseph brought the Child Jesus into the Temple, the Spirit inwardly revealed to her who He was.

The same Holy Spirit will reveal to the modern prophet who fasts and prays that Jesus Christ has come indeed as the Messiah and lives within him and lives in each human being, suffering with Him as He builds up His Body for the full glory. As he suffers, he already rejoices. As he dies, he is constantly being raised by Christ unto a new unity in love with each human being he encounters. Fasting is a death; it is also a resurrection!

6

The Prophet Prays

"Which in other ages was not made known unto the sons of men, as it is now revealed unto His holy apostles and prophets by the Spirit" (Eph. 3:5).

Karl Rahner once wrote that mysticism is one of the normal and natural things in Christian experience which no one can avoid. Even if he overlooks it, ignores it or does not understand it, it is always there as a potential spiritual experience of varying intensity and duration. Man to be truly human must always transcend himself. He must stretch upward in spirit toward the infinite.

Prayer is the prophet's key to transcendence. Prayer is his means of entering into timelessness. Prayer is a becoming! Prayer is waiting! As the prophet learns to pray, he learns how to wait upon the Lord and His good pleasure. Hence prayer is stillness! Prayer is hunger!

Prayer raises the prophet's consciousness to this primal experience of being grasped by God and known personally by Him so that in the process of being renewed, a whole new spiritual revolution takes place in his life. It is the beginning of putting on a new nature as St. Paul describes: "And be renewed in the spirit of your mind. And that you put you on the new man, which after God is created in righteousness and true holiness" (Eph. 4:23–24).

Prayer is a daily celebration in the life of the prophet of being loved by God and totally possessed by Him. He rejoices each day with Him who is born more fully in him each time he turns consciously to prayer. It becomes a joyful foretaste of the glory that awaits all of us in the life to come.

> And not only they, but ourselves also who have the first fruits of the Spirit, even we ourselves groan within ourselves, waiting for the adoption, that is, the redemption of our body (Rom. 8:23).

What must the prophet do in order to pray? He must learn daily to live on a new dimension of communication. He learns that the primary dimension of Christian prayer is receiving; it is learning to listen. In prayer the prophet enters into that total presence and relationship with God. He learns to listen to God as He loves him and he learns that he is listened to also.

How sad it is to know that so many Christians, after receiving Baptism, have lost this initial experience of the presence of God. In reality day by day, this experience should be growing, as we surrender more and more to the Spirit working in us. "That He would grant you according to the riches of His glory to be strengthened with might by His Spirit in the inner man" (Eph. 3:16).

CRISIS IN PRAYER

Today we find among all Christians a great crisis in prayer. Most people including people of prayer by profession, contemplative men and women, are totally dissatisfied with their own personal prayer life. This dissatisfaction can be the beginning of a breakthrough unto a new level of deeper prayer. Only when we are totally crushed can the Spirit do His work in us. Sanctification is the work of the Spirit, along with growth in prayer.

The prophet can and must dispose himself, but it is truly God alone who has to do the refining of our weak human nature. The prophet consents to take the first step into the wilds of the desert. He begins this journey inwardly when he answers the call to go into the inner cave, into his heart where he is freed of many of the pre-conditionings of his past life of the senses, emotions and intellect to stand before God in open confrontation with Him as the Ground of one's being.

Growth in prayer in terms of a process of growth is the very growth in this consciousness of the abiding sense and presence of God and His ever increasing assimilating activity through His love for us. For the prophet, prayer becomes this very act of continual contemplation. It is a basic standing before God where man recognizes his poverty, his sinfulness, yet is open to receive all that the Father wishes to give him. He is not praying with one faculty of his being nor is he content with focusing upon one facet of God's being. But his whole being is absorbed into the Being of his Creator. There is an experience of being "begotten" as the Word, the Son of God, is begotten by the Father. There is also a response through the Spirit of Love of his whole being back to God.

God has put into all of us this basic urge to turn toward Him. It should therefore be as natural as looking on the face of the person we love. This gaze on God is the essential act of contemplative prayer. It transcends mere self-satisfying thoughts or sentiments. It partakes more of a continual conscious communion with the Indwelling Presence within and around us.

The end of the Incarnation is precisely that God's
divine life may be restored within man's inner being by
Jesus Christ entering within man's spiritual soul by grace.
Man desires hungrily to possess this inner presence of Jesus
as light in a more conscious, unifying way. As man grows
in deeper silencing of his "heart" and begins to see how
bound he is by shadow and darkness, by sense pleasures
and false values, in such a state of alienation, he cries
continually to see more of Christ's light, to experience
more and more His assimilating presence that will bridge
the abyss separating sinful man from Him in a union of
loving surrender. Jesus Christ, the light of the world,
makes Himself "seen" within the prophet.

The prophet realizes that he cannot, by his own
powers, reach this level of "seeing" God within. No one
can teach him, nor can he teach it to someone else. Only
God can reveal it to him in experience. God is the total
source of man's being. Contemplation is therefore not a
conversation with words between the prophet and God,
but it is life lived on its deepest level. It is an immersion,
an assimilation into God's very being. "Light from light."
Our Heaven begins even now on this earth by the degree of
contemplation, of worship, of true dying to self and rising
to a Christian self-surrender, a giving of the prophet's
whole self back to Christ and through Him to render praise
and glory to God the Father. The prophet's deep, interior
prayer is an act of total surrender to the God of his life.

The prophet knows that like Moses before him, he
must pursue God up the mountain. But to begin this
journey up the mountain, he must be ready to strip
himself of excess baggage. Few become genuine prophets
because few have the courage to discipline themselves. God
calls us to climb up to Him by breaking first from all

worldly attachments to material possessions and human affections of parents, relatives and friends to be turned totally toward God's call. We need a vigilant "sobriety," a state of standing mentally vigilant, attentive to the attacks of the Evil One who seeks to turn us aside from God's call to greater union.

This stripping accompanies the prophet all the way up the long sinuous path leading to the top of the mountain into the embrace of God. He learns as he experiences more deeply God's abiding presence and His energizing love within him how to give up all attachment to lesser desires and loves in order to love only God and to find in Him all other loves.

As he grows in the consciousness of this Indwelling Presence in the deepest center of his being, at the same time he becomes conscious of this same presence in, surrounding and penetrating all other things. Like St. Francis of Assisi after his conversion, he lives on a new plateau with always a single thought of God's presence that fills him with peace and assurance. His security is within himself. Yet he finds also the same energizing, loving God without, in every creature that the prophet encounters along the path to the summit. God is no longer an object far away or a vague concept. He is a dynamic, creative force creating the prophet and the whole world around him into "receptacles of God's goodness," as St. Irenaeus of the third century describes man and other creatures.

The prophet knows with a certainty that God is very present to him. He knows with peace and assurance that he has been gifted by the humility of a loving, condescending God to attain this oneness with God and the world.

There is no more anxiety, only a growing childlike abandonment to the sacrament of the present moment as he develops a kind of global sense of God's presence everywhere. He knows that God is truly guiding him from within. As that modern prophet, Corrie Tee Boom, describes in her book, "Tramp for the Lord," the prophet knows God is directing all, giving to him that great affinity with other human beings and with all God's creatures. We could call it a breakthrough in consciousness, a phrase that aptly expresses this experience that is so important in which the prophet can grow.

In such a state of reverence towards the omnipresent God in all of creation, to think, to reflect becomes almost a waste of time for the prophet. He has learned through being quiet that he need only to rest, to wait, to breathe in the loving presence of God. His solitude is no longer solitude for he lives constantly and vividly in the presence of the Trinity. St. Symeon, the great Byzantine mystic (+1022), writes powerfully of such a prophetic vision of God indwelling the mystic in his beautiful *Hymn 27*:

> This is what it means to live completely alone.
> Because you are united with your God and King, you are
>   not alone, but you have become numbered among all
>   the Saints.
> You share a life similar to that of angels and you co-dwell
>   with the just.
> You are really the co-heir of all who are in Heaven.
> . . .For the Father and the Spirit are united with my Christ.
> How, therefore, can we speak of being a solitary when a
>   monk is united with the Three as one?
> . . .But he, who makes a heaven of his cell through virtue,
>   contemplates and looks upon the Creator of Heaven and
>   earth, installed in his cell.

And he adores Him and is united always with the Light
   that never sets, the Light without the darkness of
   evening, the unapproachable Light, which never
   leaves him, never completely wanders far from him,
   day or night, whether he eats or drinks, not even in his
   sleep or on the road or in moving from place to
   place.
And as he lives, so he dies, or, rather, even more clearly,
   the Light is united with him completely in his
   soul eternally.
. . .Only such then are monks and solitaries, those who
   alone live with God alone and in God, stripped both of
   every kind of reflection and of rationalization, see only
   God in a mind that is without thought, fixed on the
   light, as an arrow in the wall, or as a star in the heavens
   or—I fail to express it.
. . .They are not on this earth even if they are still held
   here, but they live where the angels dwell.
. . .O Marvel! As angels and as sons of the Most High,
   they will be after death gods united with God.

God appears to the prophet everywhere. Everything
shouts out to him: "Fall down and adore your Maker. The
King of Glory passes by!" In the words of Teilhard de
Chardin in his *Divine Milieu*: "Jesus Christ is shining
diaphanously through the whole world for those who have
the eyes to see!" Everything created by God is good.
Everything serves the modern prophet as a springboard
from which he is hurled towards God. People, places, his
daily contacts, at work, social gatherings, with his family,
in church, his mind plunges into the inner, intimate depths
of things and finds God always as the inner principle that
sustains all creatures in being.

"On subway walls and tenement halls" the prophet
discovers that it is in the ordinary things of life that he is
most able to "experience" a sense of true freedom to

adore God present in all things, completely and totally. Once he begins to experience God in this way he soon learns he is free because he has everything. He is touching the core of reality.

Victor Hugo once wrote:

> In the tree is a bird
> That swings
> And sings
> because it has wings.

The prophet of prayer has spiritual wings that don't lift him out of this material world in a religion of escapism, but rather that allow him to fly deeper, right into the "heart of the matter." There he finds Jesus Christ, the Evolver of this universe. The Cosmic Christ is drawing the prophet into His action of "recapitulating" the whole universe back to the Father by bringing it into its fullness through man's creative cooperation.

Prayer is ultimately a loving communion with God. Hence it admits always of a new beginning. We cannot love God today with the love of yesterday. One must be willing to bend to the ever new beginning in his life of being present to God. The prophet who prays knows he is always taking a risk, being uprooted, a pilgrim always searching for the "absent God" who becomes present when he is ready to lose today's hold on His presence. He never knows what is going to be asked of him next. The prophet never can close himself off from God's amazing revelation of Himself in the most "ungodly" situations. There is poetry in the heart of a prophet as he runs throughout this world seeking the One he loves. But still the absence and the darkness, the holding and communion and the losing and searching allow for a continual growing, a union that is almost a continual consciousness of being one with Him in whom all things have their being.

St. Paul speaks of "being in labor" until Christ is formed in us. The prophet's reality of Christ grows daily as he becomes present to the reality of Christ within, transforming him. He truly believes that Christ is incarnating Himself in his life and this very thought is an occasion for constant adoration and thanksgiving. He is given new eyes, new ears, a new heart and a new mind. In other words, his life becomes pregnant with the reality of Christ.

One reason why so many lose or do not attain this spiritual maturity is the fact that they have not maintained a spirit of quiet listening. "In quietness and confidence shall be your strength" (Is. 30:15). St. Peter confirms this when he writes:

> But let it be the hidden man of the heart, in that which is not corruptible, even the ornament of a meek and quiet spirit, which is in the sight of God of great price (1 Pet. 3:4).

Prayer is truly a listening to God that is done in a spirit of quiet receptivity to His presence and love everywhere. As pilgrim prophets we must be stripped and be poor and detached of all egoism. Christianity begins, as St. Paul tells us in Ephesians 1 and 2, with God having done everything in Christ Jesus. We must first sit and listen to all God has done for us and is doing in Christ Jesus, both within our hearts and outside ourselves in every part of God's world. There will be time for the prophet, as Elijah did, to walk, but only after we have sat and listened to the Word speak to us of the Father's great love for us.

"And he has raised us up together and made us sit together in heavenly places in Christ Jesus" (Eph. 2:6).

The prophet learns to pray by experiencing God as loving energy both within and without himself. This means he learns to stop doing and creating his own world and yields to the mind of God, "in whom are hidden all the treasures of wisdom and knowledge" (Col. 2:3).

7

The Prophet Adores God in His Heart

"But thou, when thou prayest, enter into thine inner chamber and, having shut thy door, pray to thy Father who is in secret and thy Father who sees in secret shall recompense thee" (Matt. 6:6).

We read in Holy Scripture often that Jesus went aside in silence to pray to His Heavenly Father. The disciples had surely seen Him wrapt in the glory of His Father, communing with Him in total adoration and complete self-surrender. Above all, they believed that His great power to preach mightily God's word and to heal all types of sicknesses and to perform all sorts of miracles came from His intimate communion with the Father. "The Father that dwells in Me, He does the works" (Jn. 14:10).

The modern prophet, like the disciples, goes to Jesus and asks to be taught how to pray as He prayed to His Heavenly Father.

And it came to pass, as He was praying in a certain place, that when He ceased, one of His disciples said to Him, 'Lord, teach us to pray' (Lk. 11:1).

Jesus is all turned in prayer toward the Father. "The Father is in Me and I in Him" (Jn. 10:38). He is totally related to the Father. He knows that He has come from the Father and that He goes constantly back to the Father

(Jn. 8:14). From the Father, the Source of all His being, Jesus is His unique Self: the Divine Son. He is the Word being constantly spoken by the Father; the perfect echo going back in complete harmony and submission in love to the Father by doing always the will of Him who sent Him.

Yet Jesus in prayer is also turned toward man whom He wishes to bring into that life of His Father. "I am come that they might have life and that they might have it more abundantly" (Jn. 10:10). "And this is life eternal that they might know Thee, the only true God and Jesus Christ, whom Thou hast sent" (Jn. 17:3).

In prayer the prophet begins to experience through the power of Jesus' Spirit how to enter into prayer which is truly to enter into the living relationship with Jesus Christ towards the Father as His sons and co-heirs of Heaven forever.

PRAY TO THE FATHER IN SECRET

Jesus teaches His modern prophets that if they are to be turned to their Heavenly Father and toward their brothers as well in prayer they must turn aside, put aside all superficial prayer and enter into their "inner chamber" to meet the Father. This secret meeting place is called frequently in Scripture man's "heart." It means more than the center of our emotions; it is more the "core of our being," the center of our personality. It is here, beyond the impulsiveness of our senses, emotions and even intellectual life, in that stilling of all our powers into an integrated human being that one is focused in loving adoration and surrender to the Heavenly Father.

In a beautiful meditation composed by an unknown monk of the 13th century, man's heart is likened to the tomb from which came forth the Risen Savior:

In me, in my most interior Jesus is present. All outside of our heart is only to discover the treasure hidden interiorly in the heart. There is found the sepulcher of Easter and there the new life. 'Woman, why do you weep? Whom do you seek? Whom you seek, you already possess and you do not know Him? You have the true, eternal joy and still you weep? It is more intimate to your being and still you seek it outside! You are there, outside, weeping near the tomb. Your heart is my tomb. And I am not there dead, but I repose there, living always. Your soul is My garden. You are right when you believed that I was the gardener. I am the New Adam. I work and supervise My paradise. Your tears, your love, your desire, all this is My work. You possess Me at the most intimate level of your being, without knowing it and this is why you seek Me outside. It is then outside also that I appeared to you and also that I make you to return to yourself, to make you find at the intimacy of your being, Him whom you seek outside.

The Jerusalem Bible translates the proverb: "Son, give Me thy heart" (Prov. 23:26), as "Attend to Me; keep your eyes fixed on My advice." It means a total surrender to God's inner presence of man where he is most "himself."

Jesus taught His disciples not to pray with the ostentation of the Pharisees. They were to pray "in secret." How difficult for Christians to give up the false masks that we put up before others and even before God to impress them with the Christians of prayer that we would like to be instead of presenting ourselves to the Father in utter emptiness and honesty. God is hardly seeking from us fancy speeches and spiritual poses.

Jeremiah preached to the Israelites the necessity of "circumcision of the heart." God wants to draw all of us into an interior change of heart, but as Jeremiah found:

> I hearkened and heard but they spoke not aright. No man repented of his wickedness, saying, 'What have I done?' Everyone turned to his course as the horse rushes into the battle (Jer. 8:6).

If man is to experience God deeply as his Savior, he must dedicate himself to God without reserve. It is precisely the "heart" of man that God wants, the deepest part. "For Yahweh's sake, be circumcised, remove the foreskins of your hearts" (Jer. 4:4). But it is really God who is always giving us the grace to make this personal decision of surrender totally to His dominion.

> I will give them a heart to know Me, that I am the Lord. And they shall be My people. And I will be their God. For they shall return unto me with their whole heart (Jer. 24:7).

Going into the inner chamber in secret before the Father is for the modern prophet to be totally transparent to God. He looks him through and through and knows all of his thoughts, what is truly in his "heart" (Ps. 139). Like St. Paul, the prophet can relax, putting away all pretense and all pressures from the opinions of others and from any self-judgment. "The Lord is my judge" (1 Cor. 4:4).

The prophet learns that in his "heart" he is most free. No power of the devil can touch this inner fortress. Not even haunting past memories can hinder man's desire to surrender himself in his "heart" to God. Such prayer makes man into what God has always wanted him to be: a loving, adoring son. It is in such freedom that the prophet learns how "to worship the Father in spirit and truth" (Jn. 4:24).

One of the earliest teachings that Jesus gave on prayer was to the Samaritan woman. Here was a woman hardly leading a deep, interior commitment to God. She had slaked her passionate thirst at the well of human lust and now was asking Jesus for life-giving water that would take away her thirst. Jesus tells us through this teaching that the Father seeks worshippers, those whom the Divine Word, Jesus Christ, was leading to the Father.

> The hour comes and now is, when the true worshippers shall worship the Father in spirit and truth. For such does the Father seek to be His worshippers. God is a Spirit. And they that worship Him must worship Him in spirit and truth (Jn. 4:23–2,4).

To worship in spirit and truth means more than to pray sincerely. It is a whole new relationship to the Father brought about in the Christian prophet of prayer through Jesus Christ. His great mission is to lead us to the Father in a spiritual worship that is united with His worship. Only through Him can we be taught how to worship the Father fittingly as sons. Only the Son can teach us adopted sons through grace how to please the Father.

Jesus tells us that God is a Spirit. He is beyond the altar of Mount Gerazim and the Temple in Jerusalem. He transcends all space and time. Worship by the Christian prophet can and should take place in every place at all times. There are no special times only when God can be worshipped; no special places that guarantee true worship of the Father. Above all, man's body is through Jesus Christ a temple of the Holy Spirit (1 Cor. 6:19). That Holy Spirit is given by Christ. The Spirit makes us children of the Father, capable of crying out, Abba, Father (Rom. 8:15; Gal. 4:6). We do not know how to pray properly, "in the spirit and truth," but "the Spirit also helps our infirmities. For we know not what we should pray for as we ought. But the Spirit Himself makes intercession for us with groanings which cannot be uttered" (Rom. 8:26).

PRAYER IN THE SPIRIT

The Holy Spirit dwelling within the prophet teaches him how to pray deeply in the heart. He bears witness to the prophet's spirit that he is a son of God. He teaches him a new language of praise and worship. He prepares the heart for deeper prayer and more intimate union with the Father through Jesus Christ by purifying the heart through a constant spirit of repentance. The Spirit leads the prophet into his heart where an abiding sense of sorrow for sins and fear of ever losing the loving mercy of God creates a contrite, humble heart. Broken in the spirit of egoism and independence, the prophet humbly turns in his poverty toward God. Stripped of his own power to heal himself, the prophet cries out for healing and the Spirit brings it about on the deepest level of man's being, in his "heart."

The greatest work of the Holy Spirit teaching man to pray in spirit and truth is to convict the prophet by a deep, personal experience that he truly is a son of God, divinized by grace, made a participator of the divine nature (2 Pet. 1:4). The sanctifying Spirit makes the prophet become what Jesus Christ is by nature. He truly divinizes him, regenerating man with God's very own life.

To further this divinization process the Holy Spirit continually reveals to the prophet a deeper meaning, the inner meaning of the Word of God as revealed in Holy Scripture. He opens to the Christian the treasures of the mysteries of faith. He teaches the prophet all that he needs to know about the Father and His Son, Jesus Christ.

The Holy Spirit makes it possible now for the prophet not only to know what it means to be a son of God, but He enlightens him how to translate this dignity into life at each moment. The fruit of the Holy Spirit pours over the prophet in prayer and in life's action filling him with "love, joy, peace, longsuffering, gentleness, goodness, faith, meekness, temperance" (Gal. 5:22).

The prophet therefore cries out constantly for greater release of the Holy Spirit in order to pray as he should in the Holy Trinity. He is assured by the words of Jesus Himself that if he asks, the Heavenly Father will pour out abundantly His Spirit of love upon him. "How much more shall your Heavenly Father give the Holy Spirit to them that ask Him?" (Lk. 11:13).

CONTEMPLATING THE HOLY TRINITY

The Holy Spirit, sent into the prophet's heart by the Father through Jesus Christ, comes to seize him and to give him to the Son while the Son leads him to the Father dwelling with Him in the heart of the prophet. The riches of the mystery of God are inexhaustible like an abyss. As the prophet begins to contemplate under the Holy Spirit the depths of the beauties and the love of the Trinity, Father, Son and Holy Spirit, he begins to experience what St. Paul wrote:

> May you be able to comprehend with all the saints what is the breadth and length and depth and height; and to know the love of Christ which passes knowledge that you might be filled with all the fullness of God (Ephes. 3:18–19).

To pray is to become conscious of the new relationships between the Father, Son and Holy Spirit and the individual human being praying. It is to let oneself enter into the very movement of triadic life. In deep prayer of the heart the prophet does not stop with certain feelings, affections of thoughts. He moves even beyond pictures and images and even words. The Fathers of the desert constantly exhort the one who wishes to learn how to pray to "force your mind to descend from the head to the heart and hold it there" (*St. Gregory Sinaite*).

Here the prophet is at the heart of transforming prayer. He waits in silence upon God's Word to lead him further into knowledge that is beyond human knowledge, into darkness that is true seeing. Only the Holy Spirit can reveal an experience of this divine triadic love. God is love (1 Jn. 4:8) means that He is a community of Persons loving. His very being, His existence is to love. For God to be is to love. It means that God is constantly leaving Himself to give Himself to and to exist in Another. Each person of the Trinity exists in relationship towards Another. God is Father in relationship to the Son. Jesus exists and lives only in and for the Father to whom He gives Himself entirely. Their mutual love expresses itself in a procession of Personified Love, the Holy Spirit. To pray in the heart is to experience this immense circulation of love among the Persons within the divine family.

Touching the heart of the Trinity the prophet is truly at the source of love in the world and the Church. When Jesus gave His most important commandments to love God and neighbor (Matt. 23:34–40) He did nothing but to situate His disciples at the heart of the Trinity. In contemplating the Trinity, the prophet experiences a love which comes from on high and unites intimately the three Divine Persons dwelling within him. "The love of God is shed abroad in our hearts by the Holy Spirit who is given unto us" (Rom. 5:5).

The prophet experiences in this divine love poured into his heart a double movement. He receives the gift of

God's love which is the giving of the Father, Son and Holy Spirit to the prophet. And there follows a reciprocity, a return giving of self back to the Trinity. The prophet can enter into this current of Trinitarian love only on condition that he surrenders to that divine love, totally dispossessing himself in utter poverty to give himself to God and to others.

The prophet understands how love of the Holy Trinity means love of his neighbor. Gazing on the flaming love of the Father, Son and Holy Spirit within him, he is impelled outwardly by this very Trinitarian love to reproduce the same selfgiving of the Trinity to others outside.

LOVE TOWARDS OTHERS

The paradox of true love towards the Trinity is that the more the Christian prophet is swept into a unity of "being" in the Trinity, the more he is impelled by that very interior Trinitarian life to move outwardly to establish by his love for his neighbors a community of self-giving persons. Teilhard de Chardin insists that love differentiates as it unites. As the Trinity brings the Christian into a sense of "belonging," of being brought into the very family of the Trinity, this sense of unity gives the individual a new-founded sense of individuation. He knows through a deep, abiding experience that he is being constantly loved by the three divine Persons, Father, Son and Holy Spirit. He knows himself as an *I* loved by three Persons, each a *Thou*.

Such an *I* is now capable of giving himself to others. He has an identity that no one can ever take from him. He may be slighted, insulted, rejected, even hated by others.

Yet he stands firm because he knows who he is. He knows from whom he has come and to whom he must go. He is not mercurial, changing his moods, attitudes and convictions according to the opinions of other men around him. Still he is humble and a loving servant towards all.

He is thus because in deep prayer of the heart he has discovered the Trinity as the ground of his own being and at the same time he discovers the Triune God as the most intimate bond of all creation. The creative energies found in each person giving that person his uniqueness is the very presence of the Trinity living and loving in him.

Thus the prophet of prayer realizes a synthesis between the commandment to love God above all else and the commandment to love one another. True love for God will engender the strongest love for others. For it will be ultimately the loving presence of the Trinity within him that will be the force behind his own human love for others. There is only one source of true love, divine or human, and that is found ultimately in the Trinity.

> Let us love one another. For love is of God and everyone that loves is born of God and knows God. He that loves not knows not God for God is love. . .If we love one another, God dwells in us and His love is perfected in us. . .God is love and he that dwells in love dwells in God and God in him (1 Jn. 4:7–16).

Such a prophet, drawn to the world, becomes more and more aware that with St. Paul he has been called to bring all things through Jesus Christ unto the Father in the Spirit of love. "And all things are of God who has reconciled us to Himself by Jesus Christ and has given us the ministry of reconciliation" (2 Cor. 5:18). He is an "ambassador of Christ" called to love the Lord God with his whole heart and to love all other creatures in Him.

The final test of true prayer, whether it is authentic and of a deep, personalistic encounter with God, must consist in man's ability to love others as God has loved us. He discovers this powerful love of the Trinity within himself. And he finds that same love permeating all of creation, especially in other human beings made according to God's own image. He seeks to draw out that God-life in each person encountered. He serves the best in each person because he knows that is man in his transcendent openness to the indwelling Trinity. He moves through this world with deep peace and joy, content to love and serve each person that God offers him to minister His healing love to through the human love the prophet shows to the other.

God's love is incarnated in human form, not only in Jesus Christ, the Word-Incarnate, but through His resurrectional presence living within the modern prophet by grace, this love touches other human beings and draws them also into the salvific love of God Himself. Prayer is ultimately the prophet gazing upon the Father's countenance, receiving his whole life as a gift from Him and returning it back to the Father through Jesus Christ and the Holy Spirit. But in that gaze and gift and return of that gift the prophet also finds God as the Giver of life to all creatures. By the divine love dwelling within him, he is able at each moment to offer in humble service to the other the whole, wonderful world of human beings and all non-human creatures back to God in prayerful worship. But it is now the worship of a community of creatures praising together their Creator who has brought forth all things through His Son Jesus Christ and His Holy Spirit and in them through the praying prophet brings them all into their fullness.

8

The Prophet Thirsts

"They wandered in the wilderness in a solitary way. They found no city to dwell in. Hungry and thirsty, their soul fainted in them. Then they cried unto the Lord in their trouble and He delivered them out of their distresses" (Ps. 107:4—6).

Anyone who has wandered in the hot, arid desert with no water knows what a maddening thirst can consume him. Day and night he thinks only of clear, sweet, cool water that will give him new life.

The prophet who has the courage to enter deeply into the interior desert of his own poverty knows well what a thirst for God means. He cries out in the words of the Psalmist who surely knew the burning thirst in his soul when he began to seek God, found Him and then lost Him:

O God, Thou art my God; early will I seek Thee. My soul thirsts for Thee, my flesh longs for Thee in a dry and thirsty land where no water is. To see Thy power and Thy glory, so as I have seen Thee in the sanctuary. Because Thy loving kindness is better than life, my lips shall praise Thee (Ps. 63:1—3).

One who has not begun to taste and to see how sweet the Lord is will not seek Him with a burning thirst described in *Psalm 42:*

As the heart pants after the water brooks, so pants my soul after Thee, O God. My soul thirsts for God, for the living God. When shall I come and appear before God? My tears have been my meat day and night, while they continually say unto me: 'Where is thy God?' (Ps. 42:1–3).

Prayer is man standing in the desert, hungry and thirsty, stretching out with the totality of his being to possess God as the source of his being. He has tried the pleasures of this world and, like a child who gleefully stretches out to grasp the beautifully colored soap bubbles, he stands on the brink of despair with a handful of nothingness.

The desert teaches the prophet that God has made him for Himself. Nothing in the whole world will ever satisfy him but God. In having God, then he will truly not only possess the whole world but he will come into the true possession of himself. God has given man this basic drive to possess Him. And there never has existed the human being who found full self-actualization in the possession of material things or even in the love for certain human beings.

God created man "according to His image and likeness" (Gen. 1:26). In this ongoing creation, the development of these seeds of divinity in each human being to become a child of God, man finds his greatest dignity. He is being called into the desert of this world to receive the Word in whom he will understand his true dignity to be with the Son of God also a son of the same Father. When man steps into the silence of the desert, he knows what Emil Brunner says is true: "The being of man as an 'I' is being from and in the Divine 'Thou,' or more exactly, from and in the Divine Word, whose claim 'calls' man's being into existence." God is calling man always to consent to be swept up into the Trinitarian life and he alone can reply. His answer fulfills the purpose for which he was made or he destroys himself as a human being.

Such a spiritual thirst, therefore, is at the heart of being truly human. It is a yearning to become "whole." It longs that the image of God in man reach its full fruition. Many human beings thirst for God only when they have fallen to the depths of human degradation and emptiness. Others thirst for God because through the gift of prayer God has revealed Himself in a partial vision of His perfect beauty along with a vivid experience of their own emptiness apart from God.

But thirst is the biblical sensation that best describes what God's prophet experiences as he begins to grow in union with God. How can he truly experience God's beauty and not want more? Like the Bride in the *Song of Songs*, the prophet in the desert cries out:

> Let him kiss me with the kisses of his mouth; for thy love is better than wine. Because of the savor of thy good ointments thy name is as ointment poured forth, therefore do the virgins love thee. Draw me, we will run after thee. The king has brought me into his chambers. We will be glad and rejoice in thee. We will remember thy love more than wine. The upright love thee (Song of Songs: 1:1—4).

St. Paul burned with such a thirst to "put on Christ," to suffer with Him that he might be glorified forever with Him. He knew he was one in Christ Jesus; yet something of Paul's thirst comes through the ardent words he uses to describe his stretching out to possess still more Jesus Lord.

> I count myself not to have apprehended; but this one thing I do, forgetting those things which are behind and reaching forth unto those things which are before, I press toward the mark for the prize of the high calling of God in Christ Jesus (Phil. 3:13—14).

In Greek the word Paul uses is *epekteinomenos*. The Greek prefix, *ep(i)*, suggests a dynamic, energetic pouncing upon of an ardently desired good. The prefix, *ek*, hints at some movement from outside, a hungry desire to possess the Unpossessable. Out of this concept of Paul's stretching forward, straining toward a greater possession of God, St. Gregory of Nyssa builds a mystical theology as he describes it in his *Life of Moses* around the theme of *epectasis*, a burning desire in the heart of man to possess ever more God as his sole love.

On Gregory's commentary on the *Song of Songs*, he describes the thirst of the prophet in the desert:

> The soul, that looks up towards God and conceives that good desire for His eternal beauty, constantly experiences an ever new yearning for that which lies ahead and her desire is never given its full satisfaction.

The Christian prophet in the desert, much like the Samaritan adulteress at the well of Jacob, thirsts for the living water that is Jesus Christ. Holy Scripture promises this living water that would take away any further thirsting. "I will give unto him that is athirst of the fountain of the water of life freely" (Rev. 21:6). The Lamb of God is to lead the thirsty to fountains of living water (Rev. 7:17). The Prophet Isaiah gives the promise that the Chosen People would draw water with joy from the wells of salvation. "Therefore with joy shall you draw out of the wells of salvation" (Is. 12:3). Again the same prophet foretells:

> For I will pour water upon him that is thirst and floods upon the dry ground. I will pour My Spirit upon thy seed and My blessing upon thy offspring (Is. 44:3).

> This drink would be free. One has only to thirst and come to drink.

Everyone that thirsts, come you to the waters and he that has no money, come, buy and eat. Yes, come, buy wine and milk without money and without price (Is. 55:1).

God freely gives this quenching drink to all who wish to come and drink. But the Prophet Jeremiah lamented that people had forsaken God, "the fountain of living waters" (Jer. 2:13) and hewed for themselves broken cisterns that could hold no water.

Still the Prophet Ezekiel had the vision of the future river of living water. He walked into the water that gradually covered him; it became a river that he could not pass over, "waters to swim in, a river that could not be passed over" (Ezek. 47:5) yet waters that would heal all illnesses. Zechariah also saw in the new world a cleansing fountain opening up to all sick and needy (Zech. 13:1).

Jesus Christ claims to a thirsty woman that He is the Messiah, the One who can give "living water" that will take away any thirst for lesser goods, unsatisfying pleasures, imitation beauty. Before the modern prophet can lead others to this "living water," he must first drink from it in his heart that the desert of sin and his own poverty have raised to a feverish panting. He knows, as he drinks of Jesus Lord that only in Him is true Life. He dies to self in a living baptism in which the living waters of Jesus Christ's life-giving presence surround him completely and heal him of all sickness. These waters refresh and give full life. Such a prophet then can bring the thirsty to drink of this same "living water."

COME TO ME ALL WHO THIRST

The prophet, because he has drunk deeply of this saving water that is Jesus Christ, can point out to others to

come and drink also. He has heard the beautiful words that
St. John records which Jesus Christ cried out to the thirsty
crowds in Jerusalem on the Festival of Tabernacles or
Booths.

> In the last day, that great day of the feast, Jesus stood and
> cried, saying: 'If any man thirst, let him come unto Me and
> drink. He that believes in Me as the Scripture has said, out of
> his belly shall flow rivers of living water.' But this He spoke of
> the Spirit whom they that believe in Him should receive. For
> the Holy Spirit was not yet given, because Jesus was not yet
> glorified (Jn. 7:37–39).

This beautiful feast recalled each year the time that
the Israelites had been homeless wanderers in the desert
without a roof over their heads (Lev. 23: 40–43). The
Jews were to build booths of temporary structure that
would give protection from the weather but would not
shut out the sun. At night they would be able to see the
stars through the thatched roof overhead. At the climax of
this feast, a priest brought a golden pitcher filled with
water from the Pool of Siloam and poured it out on the
altar as an offering to God while the people recited the
words from Isaiah 12:3: "With joy shall you draw water
out of the wells of salvation." The people thanked God for
life-giving water.

It was probably at this solemn moment that Jesus
Christ stood up and invited the world to drink of the living
water that He would give them. He had told the Samaritan
woman: "The water that I shall give him shall be in him a
well of living water springing up into everlasting life" (Jn.
4:14). Now He was inviting all men to partake of the
life-giving waters that would flow from inside a man, deep
down in the depths of his being, where the Holy Spirit of

Jesus Christ would dwell. Jesus promises to the modern prophet who thirsts in the desert that He will put deep down into the very bowels of man's being His Spirit of Love who will lead us into a new knowledge and wisdom and understanding that Jesus is Lord and that with Him we have a loving Father who calls us into being His loving children.

St. Paul used the image of the rock that Moses struck and from it flowed forth living, life-giving waters to refer to Jesus Christ (Exod. 17:6; I Cor. 10:4). "And all did drink the same spiritual drink, for they drank of that spiritual Rock that followed them. And that Rock was Christ."

Jesus the Rock still stands in the midst of the desert of life inviting all to come and drink of His life-giving Spirit. The prophet comes and drinks because he has been thirsting all his life for this water. As he slakes his thirst, as the life-giving water soothes all parts of his weary being, he experiences a deep contentment and strength.

Yet the prophet of deep prayer in the desert knows a paradoxical unrest. Although he is refreshed by this water, he cannot get enough of it. He knows he must journey on. Yet he knows also he carries this life-giving water within himself. The mystery of union with Jesus Christ, the fullness of God's perfection, is that the more one drinks of Him the more one desires to drink deeper. There is generated a fire that soothes and gives joy and contentment that God loves him, yet the contemplative burns to be turned totally into the light of Jesus Christ.

St. Symeon the New Theologian (+1022) beautifully expresses this experience of receiving the Holy Spirit through Jesus Christ that generates again a burning longing for greater union.

If a man who possesses within him the light of the Holy Spirit, is unable to bear its radiance, he falls prostrate on the ground and cries out in great fear and terror, as one who sees and experiences something beyond nature, above words or reason. He is then like a man whose entrails have been set on fire and, unable to bear the scorching flame, he is utterly devastated by it and deprived of all power to be in himself. But, through constant watering and cooling by tears, the flame of divine desire in him burns all the brighter, producing yet more copious tears and, being washed by their flow, he shines with ever greater radiance. And when the whole of him is aflame and he becomes as light, the words of John the Divine are fulfilled: 'God unites with gods and is known by them!'

Man can thank God for planting within him a thirst for Himself that is unsatiable. It is an infinity of growth which will never exhaust the potential that God has given man to be in Christ; "to put on Christ." God continually attracts with His infinite holiness and beauty man who knows in the possession already of God, more intimately to himself than he himself, as St. Augustine put it, that he has not even begun to fill the depths, to satisfy the painful thirst and hunger for more of God. Yet without such thirst and hunger he cannot live. St. Gregory of Nyssa beautifully describes this soaring towards infinity:

And thus the soul moves ceaselessly upwards, always reviving its tension for its onward flight by means of the progress it has already realized. Indeed, it is only spiritual activity that nourishes its force by exercise; it does not slacken its tension by action but rather increases it (Life of Moses).

In biblical terms thirst for living water is a powerful imagery of this desire for God. When it is satisfied however, when man is integrated into God, his potential for God is raised to a new ability to "absorb" God and be absorbed into His Being. He reaches a point of equilibrium, peaceful stability. The restlessness that Augustine speaks about in his *Confessions* that is in the prophet's heart is put at rest only in God. Yet the very resting in God sets up a new motion towards greater possession of God.

It is the Bride always losing the Bridegroom and in the search her love for him grows to greater intensity.

> By night on my bed I sought him whom my soul loves. I sought him, but I found him not. I will rise now and go about the city in the streets and in the broad wave I will seek him whom my soul loves. I sought him, but I found him not (Song of Songs 3:1–2).

The prophet in the desert comes to know through experience that not only his life on this earth but his whole spiritual existence in the life to come will consist in the joyful tension of being in God, having drunk to satisfaction from the well of living water and, still as St. Paul says, "Not yet!" He knows that to love is to thirst for deeper union with the Beloved.

Peaceful, joyful excitement that beckons him forth to a call toward greater life changes his life of sameness, banality and meaninglessness into a childlike wonderment. The more he finds God in each creature that he meets, in each moment, in each event, the more he laughingly stretches out to meet Him still more consciously, more totally.

Heaven will be the state of continuous growth in finding God in all of His wonderful creatures and wanting to lead others to discover the same God loving them as well. Thirst is one of man's primitive experiences. Remove all drink from his life and he will thirst. He will soon die if he has nothing to drink. How better to describe man's relationship towards God. He was made to thirst for God.

Yet God is always giving Himself to drink. Jesus Christ is always calling out to all who thirst, "Come to Me and I will give you living waters."

The prophet who thirsts knows that his total health and happiness consist in continually thirsting for God. The more he thirsts, the more he can drink in the allness of God's goodness, and the more also he thirsts to lead others to drink. As he offers this Living Water to the thirsty multitude, he too thirsts still more to bring the whole world to drink of his treasure. The nature of this Eternal Well is to pour its waters out to the thirsty. The Well has no bottom. It is inexhaustible. And so is the thirst of the prophet!

9

The Prophet Hopes

"Blessed be the God and Father of our Lord Jesus Christ who according to His abundant mercy has begotten us again unto a lively hope by the resurrection of Jesus Christ from the dead" (1 Pet. 1,3).

Dr. Harold Urey, one of the fathers of the atom bomb, knelt down on the flats of New Mexico when the first great mushroom exploded up into the sky and he covered his head. He said later that he had uttered a prayer to God. "I am a frightened man and the whole human race should be frightened too!" Man was coming of age to control, shape or destroy this universe, but Dr. Urey prayed to God that "hopefully man would use his new-found power properly to help and not destroy mankind."

No matter how sophisticated man may become, he will always be in need of hope. He always will be in need of a greater than himself to bring himself to completion. When man loses hope in God and in fellow man, he loses hope in himself and he will soon commit suicide. Hope is that peculiar human quality that allows us to come back day after day amidst conflicts and struggles to expect a better day than yesterday, a fuller health, more happiness, greater love than what we had attained at any time before.

But when man yields to fatalism that there is no *hope* for improvement in man's human condition, he ceases to be a human being and turns into an animal. Before Christianity the pagan Greek tragedian, Euripedes, and the Latin poet, Lucretius, both lamented a new born baby, brought into life only to suffer a bit and then to die. J. P. Sartre with his type of nihilistic existentialism scoffs in his empty hopelessness to say there is *no exit* from the absurdity of life into which every man is born. Hell, for Sartre, sardonically is "other people!"

But Christianity gives to the world a concept of *hope* that is rooted in God's fidelity. In the *Hesed* Covenant that God established first with Abraham and then through Moses with God's chosen people in the desert, God promises to become involved with His people. He condescends with His mercy which is not a concept of God with utter detachment "forgiving" the errors of His people. Mercy in the Old Testament is equivalent to St. Paul's concept of *charis* or *grace* in the New Testament. God truly seeks to give Himself at every moment of His people's existence. He will protect them and restore to them full prosperity, granting them happiness as the fulfillment of all their desires.

The chosen people responded with a confidence because they *hoped* in God. They trusted in His revealed Word. St. Paul points out that Abel, Enoch, Noah, Abraham, Isaac and Jacob believed in the Lord God. They hoped in His promises, hence were "awaiting the city with foundations whose architect and builder is God" (Hebr. 11:10).

But the fullness of human hope is shown in the revelation made to the chosen people of God through the Word made flesh, Jesus Christ. He comes to give us hope against fatalism that after human death there is no other life eternal. But more positively He comes to reveal to us the infinite love of the Heavenly Father who so loves us as to give us His only begotten Son so that whoever believes in Him will not die but will have eternal life (Jn. 3:16).

Now Jesus Christ is our hope. Man knows now that God has created him "according to the Image and Likeness" (Gen. 1:26) that is Jesus Christ. In Him is the Father's fullness.

> For in Him dwells all the fullness of the Godhead bodily. And you are complete in Him who is the head of all principality and power. . .Buried with Him in Baptism, wherein also you are risen with Him through the faith of the operation of God, who has raised Him from the dead (Col. 2:9,12).

We have no other way to know the Father but through the Son who reveals to us the Father. "He that has seen Me has seen the Father" (Jn. 14:19). Yet we most see the Father, know His dynamic, self-giving love when with St. Paul we come to the almost unbelievable good news that Jesus Christ "died for us, that whether we wake or sleep, we should live together with Him" (1 Thes. 5:10). Jesus Christ is our hope because He is the perfect Image of the Heavenly Father (Col. 1, 15). Love proves itself by deeds, by an outpouring. Paul uses the Greek word *kenosis* which means an emptying, a total outpouring, a hollowing out, to describe best the infinite love of Jesus Christ for us sinners.

> Let this mind be in you which was also in Christ Jesus who, being in the form of God, thought it not robbery to be equal with God. But He made Himself of no reputation and took upon Himself the form of a servant and was made in the likeness of men. And being found in fashion as a man, He humbled Himself and became obedient unto death, even the death of the cross. Wherefore God also has highly exalted Him and given Him a name which is above every name that at the name

of Jesus every knee should bow, of things in Heaven and things on earth and things under the earth. And that every tongue should confess that Jesus Christ is Lord to the glory of God the Father (Phil. 2:5—11).

If Jesus Christ so loved us that He emptied Himself totally of all He possessed in the terrifying "hollowing out" on the cross and He is the perfect image of the Father, then we understand a bit of how great the Father's love for us is! Jesus all of His human existence experienced as all of us have to do the love of the Father. But He was Himself the source of hope. The Divine Logos that was with the Father from the very beginning of time (Jn. 1:1) was continually being begotten by the Father at Nazareth and on the mountain top and during His preaching in His years of ministry leading to Calvary. Being so loved by the Father with an infinite *kenosis*, an infinite outpouring and emptying of the Fatherhood totally into His Son, Jesus Christ sought through the medium of His humanity to express that total surrender to the Father. "I do always those things that please Him" (Jn. 8:29).

The hideous, crushed being on the cross, this "worm and no man" (Ps. 22:6), reaches the ultimate in human expression of what divine love means. The most powerful words in Scripture are those that Jesus uttered to His beloved disciples as He was filled with this divine love on the eve of His *kenosis*: "As the Father has loved Me, so have I loved you. Continue in My love" (Jn. 15:9). The Father pours out the fullness of His infinite Being into the Son. All that the Father has the Son has. And Jesus is telling us that He has the same infinite, outpouring, emptying love for us that the Father has for Him. And we must abide in that love. We must love one another with that same type of *kenosis*, emptying of self, not in imitation of what the Father and Son have done in loving us, but in experiencing continually the abiding, loving presence of the Father and the Son in their mutual binding force of the Holy Spirit of love. As we believe in this indwelling Trinity loving in us, we can hope in the Father, Son and Holy Spirit's continued love and thus love in return with Their very love both God and our fellow-man.

Today the crucial religious problem is how to meet God. How can we come to know Him today in our urban society with circumstances so different from those in which the nomadic Israelites of the Old Testament, the early Christians of the Pauline Epistles, the Fathers in the desert, the monks in medieval monasteries?

Although the external circumstances do change and our nuclear age has radically changed our way of encountering in God as a Creator of immense energy, never static, always moving, yet there is a constant in which we *hope*. Modern prophets of hope place their hope as all Christians of all times in the unchanging revelation in Christ Jesus of God's undying, infinite love for each of us individually.

Part of our hope will always be the incompleteness in our ability to possess God. His *beyondness* and *unreachableness* by our own power will always force us to have something of the similar wild risk of trusting in God's fidelity that the faithful Israelites showed in the desert.

Whatever be the revelation made by the son Jesus Christ of the Father's love for us, whatever be the experience that we are graced by God of His abiding love within our lives, there will always be something unfathomable about God. Not even in eternity will we be able to penetrate this mysterious love of God for us. To love God really we must be prophets who hope in Him at all times, and this will always mean taking a risk in the dark, of letting go under the powerful, hidden hand of God. We hope in His love as sheep hope in the goodness and protective love of the Good Shepherd who leads them to green pastures (Ps. 23).

The life of every genuine Christian is a risk and to live in hope means to live dangerously for we stake our lives on God alone. In hope we learn to accept God in all His unfathomableness. To accept God's love for us means that, besides accepting this love of God, we respond to it, that we respond to the Person loving us. That Person is God.

The first part of that surrendering love is that we accept Him wholly and entirely. We let Him take complete possession of our lives. I cannot reach out to God, not even to accept His love unless the Holy Spirit inspires me to that belief, hope and love. The Spirit's primary grace is to inspire me to "want" God. But His gift of my wanting to possess God follows upon the most primary of all graces: that God, prior to anything else in our regard, has always been loving us. With utter freedom flowing from His holiness and absolute perfection He loves us simply because He wants to. God is love and love pours itself out. Love is always a *kenosis*, an emptying, a pouring out toward another. My faith through the power of the Holy Spirit convicts me of God's eternal love for me. This is the basis for our hope.

We hope in Him and we hope that He will give us all we need to go to Him in perfect, unfaltering love. Hope recognizes humbly our own weakness and utter inability to love God or be loving in His regard. But it places all our strength in His goodness and holiness. When we fathom something of the "unfathomableness" of God and let ourselves be abandoned to this love, that is *hope*. Hope is the unifying force between faith and love. Hope begins in the unfathomableness of God. We will never totally possess Him or control Him. We will never be able to grasp with full knowledge what God is or what He is essentially like. If we did possess this perfect knowledge of God we would be like God himself. Thus we must abandon ourselves to Him completely in hope and trust. We let go of ourselves and take the risk of letting God take complete control of our lives.

In faith I come to accept God for His love. In hope I accept God for His "unfathomableness" which will remain in varying degrees for all eternity. Something of this unfathomableness of God is shared in each person with whom we come into contact, especially those closest to us in our daily living communities. To love another person we need to enter into a similar risk of the unfathomable. We recognize the uncontrollable presence of God in the other. We do not seek to dominate God in the other. Thus we approach the other in hope, a willingness to live with the risk of not controlling all factors in human love.

The modern prophet not only calls others to let go in hope and love in order to build a community of brothers and sisters under the one same loving Father but his whole life radiates this hope towards each person he meets. He is ready to let the other person be uniquely the person God wishes him to be. More than this, he actively is working with the presence of God abiding within that person to bring that person into the fullness of God-life that God wishes to be there. The prophet has, therefore, the virginal hope of Mary, the Mother of God. It is a surrender to the mysterious working of God in innumerable incarnations in every human situation. Hope allows him to be totally at God's disposition even though the details, the whole plan of this or that moment of salvation are not known and controlled by him.

He lets God take full possession of his life. It means that he does not have any pre-conceived ideas of how God will act next in his life or in the lives of others. He reverently lets God be God! It is as simple as all that. He is totally open to God that He may speak whatever healing, loving word He wishes in his life. Too often we go to prayer anticipating the word *we* wish God to say to us. Hope in God is the reverence that allows *Him* the utter freedom to do with us whatever He wishes. We allow Him to say His word, whatever it may be and whatever it may cost us. "Behold the handmaid of the Lord. Be it done to me according to Thy word!" (Lk. 1:38).

Thomas Merton describes this waiting in prayer for the Lord to speak *His* word when He wishes and what He wishes to say. It is not a receptivity to a certain kind of message. It is a general emptying "that awaits to realize the fullness of the message of God within its own apparent void. The true contemplative. . .remains empty because he knows that he can never expect or anticipate the word that will transform his darkness into light."

The prophet of hope does not hope in his own power to tell God how to run His world or even the life of the prophet. The prophet exists only for the Lord. God can do with him whatever He wishes. The prophet lives in the inner world of God's great majesty and transcendence and in hoping surrenders himself totally to serve God.

St. Paul well describes hope as that which is unseen, yet which is most real.

For we are saved by hope, but hope that is seen is not hope. For what a man sees, why does he yet hope for? But if we hope for that which we see not, then do we with patience wait for it. (Rom. 8:24–25).

Modern prophets therefore let God plan their lives. It suffices in hope to follow God's lead, step by step, moment by moment. The promptings of the Holy Spirit tell us what to do next. We must not be anxious to force God to reveal His plan well in advance for then where is our hope? Are we letting God be the supreme God in our lives when we demand a clear path, with no darkness? He asks me now to cross this river and not to worry about the other thousands of rivers I could cross or will have to cross in the future. With hope I cross one river at a time.

Abraham was a man of great faith and hope as St. Paul tells us:

By faith Abraham, when he was called to go out into a place which he should after receive for an inheritance, obeyed; and he went out, not knowing whither he went. By faith he sojourned in the land of promise as in a strange country, dwelling in tents with Isaac and Jacob, the heirs with him of the same promise. For he looked for a city which has foundations whose builder and maker is God. (Heb. 11:9–10).

And God built upon his faith and hope the whole people of God. His children would qualify to be Abraham's children, not by blood or circumcision but by their similar abandonment to God's love and fidelity in complete belief and hope that God would be true to His word. These children, God promised, would be as numerous as the sands on the earth (Gen. 13:16).

Today, as always in time past, God is calling forth prophets who will *hope* in Him by surrendering themselves totally to His majesty, to let Him do whatever He wishes in their lives. Jesus Christ is their hope for He makes the *beyondness* and *unreachableness* of the infinite Heavenly Father a possibility of possessing in hope,without control on man's part. The oath that God swore is His Word, Jesus Christ, the New Covenant. Jesus is God's fidelity-pledge to us. Thus the prophet hopes in Christ Jesus. For this reason Paul can exhort all of us to this hope:

> Wherein God, willing more abundantly to show unto the heirs of promise the immutable things, in which it was impossible for God to live, we might have a strong consolation, who have fled for refuge to lay hold upon the hope set before us. This hope we have as an anchor of the soul, both sure and steadfast and which enters into that within the veil, whither the forerunner is for us entered, even Jesus, made aa high priest forever after the order of Melchisedec (Heb. 6:17—20).

10

The Prophet's Father

"There is one Body and one Spirit, even as you are called in the one hope of your calling; one Lord, one faith, one Baptism; one God and Father of all who is above all and through all and in you all" (Eph. 4:4–6).

Jesus Christ came on this earth to reveal to us that we have a Heavenly Father. He makes it possible through the grace of the Holy Spirit actually to become as St. Peter says, "partakers of the divine nature" (2 Pet. 1:4).

Man is born a lonely, estranged, alienated orphan. He has no true identity in a land of strangers. In his loneliness he resorts to pride and power, hatred and violence, all the sins that are signs of his assertion that he is important and worthy of being loved. Jesus Christ's redemptive work can be seen as one of not only revealing to us the Father and making it possible to become truly brothers with Him and with every other human being but His work is to give us a continued experience of this Father's love through the love He bears us. We stop sinning when we are sure of the love of the Other and that Other is God, the infinite, most perfect being for whom we have been made. Our hearts are truly restless, says St. Augustine, until they rest in God.

Christ's "imaged" love of the Father is one of identity. "As the Father has loved Me, so have I loved you" (Jn. 15:9). As we look up at the Cross and see the depths of Jesus' love for us, we should see at the same time the love of the Father. We should realize in moments of deep prayer, especially in receiving the actual Risen Lord Jesus in Holy Eucharist that the mind-set of Jesus is that of a Divine Person. There is no mutability in His surrendering act of love that reaches the climax on the Cross. He is always dying for me! He did die once historically in a place in Jerusalem on a cross on a given day. Yet, because His oblation in love for us was an act of God, His love at that same intensity remains constant and unchanging.

What Jesus does on the Cross is to "reveal" to us the infinite love of the Father. Would it be too far-fetched to imagine that when Jesus Christ cried out with joyful triumph and exultation, "It is finished!" (Jn. 19:30), "Father into Thy hands I commend My spirit!" (Lk. 23:46), He heard again those words that He had heard frequently during His earthly life: "You are My Beloved Son in whom I am well pleased. You do exactly what I would do if I had a body!"

The Incarnate Word therefore lives within us, sending us His Spirit who reveals at each moment in our lives the infinite love of *Our Father*. Through prayer and the sacrament of each moment the modern prophet grows daily under the power of the Holy Spirit in the knowledge that he has a Heavenly Father who loves and cares for him. Jesus Christ reveals to him that this Father cares for the lilies of the field and the birds of the air. He will surely care for all of us too.

> Behold the fowls of the air; for they sow not, neither do they reap nor gather into barns; yet your heavenly Father feeds them. Are you not much better than they? (Matt. 6:26–30).

He knows well also the meaning of the words: ". . .

and we all have the same God and Father who is above all and through all and in you all" (Eph. 4:6). He has a Father in Heaven who tenderly loves and cares for him in all circumstances of his life. It is this deep personal relationship with the Father that Jesus came not only to reveal but to give to us through His Holy Spirit as a constant experience.

> But the Comforter who is the Holy Spirit whom the Father will send in My name, He shall teach you all things and bring all things to your remembrance, whatsoever I have said unto you (Jn. 14:26).

The more the prophet becomes an interior man through experiencing love, the more he realizes that the whole Christian life and charismatic renewal are based on this peak experience of being loved by the Father. Man becomes most human, not when he is merely engaged in ordinary human acts such as eating, drinking and sleeping, but when he is loving in an unselfish manner. The deeper a person loves another human being in true ego-transcendence, the more immediately in that same experience does he experience the love of God the Father pouring Himself out into His Son, His Other-Self.

> No man has seen God at any time. If we love one another, God dwells in us and His love is perfected in us. . .God is love. And he that dwells in love dwells in God and God in him (1 Jn. 4:12, 16).

IN SILENCE THE FATHER SPEAKS

Just as the deepest moments of human love come in silent communion that transcends words and actions, so too the prophet learns to turn within and find that the

Father abides with His Son in him. Every man, woman and child needs to have times and moments when he can be alone to expose his poverty and neediness to the Father in Heaven. Every day becomes then a Sabbath, as one learns to spend more and more time worshipping the Father "in spirit and in truth." Prayer is this continual, conscious communion with the Source of our being.

Catherine Dougherty, the famous foundress of Madonna House, is so convinced of the need we have of a place to go to where we can be alone with the Father in silent adoration in union with Jesus Lord and His Spirit. She has established in her Canadian community the "poustyn" which in Russian means the desert. It is a cabin off in the woods where a person can sink into the silence of the Father, hear His creative love in His Son and Spirit. This stems back to her childhood in Russia where all Russian families had a white-washed corner of a room with icons, the Gospel and an oil lamp always burning. Here the Russian Christians could be alone in prayerful communion with God. She insists that all the problems in today's world can be solved if the world would only seek its time for solitude.

George Washington Carver is a model for the modern prophet. He went to his laboratory long before daylight and spent hours communing with the Heavenly Father before he began his own scientific experiments. We need time to rediscover this awesome presence of the Father. It isn't so much that we go to find God but He takes us up into Himself when we merely turn within. God says to the modern prophet just as He said long ago: "Therefore, behold, I will allure her and bring her into the wilderness and speak comfortably unto her" (Hos. 2:14).

The prophet knows that these deserts of solitude are not necessarily places but states of soul and mind. If he hungers for God he will find these deserts and solitudes almost everywhere because he realizes the tremendous need he has for such. It is really God who makes solitudes and deserts and silences to be holy moments of immersion of ourselves into Him. And in such communion we begin to see anew our relationship to the Heavenly Father.

The modern prophet recognizes his own poverty, his sinfulness and his heart continually cries out, "Abba, Father!" He will find many of his humble tasks at work or at home, waiting for stop lights or trains or planes as points of real departure where he can be alone with his Abba, Father and experience for himself the Father's great love for him.

But like every other skill, this sensitivity to the Father takes practice as the prophet learns to be so attuned to God that the moment he is alone, the Father is free to enter in and speak. True silence is not always an absence of speech, but it is the continual listening to God. The mere absence of noise in the life of a prophet is not silence. A busy day at work, teaching school or directing traffic or taking care of children at home can be a day of silence if the prophet recognizes in each event, each action, each word, each thought a specific, loving communication of the Father to him.

The prophet knows that the Father truly lives within him. St. John tells us: "God so loved the world that He gave His only begotten Son that whosoever believes in Him should not perish, but have everlasting life" (Jn. 3:16). This is not merely an historical event but it is the Father always loving us, always begetting Jesus in our lives, always sending Jesus to heal us of our blindness and sickness.

As Jesus is born into our hearts and sends us His Spirit to reveal through the Word the Fatherhood, we continually experience what Holy Scripture so clearly teaches us about the Father.

OUR FATHER IN HOLY SCRIPTURE

In portraying God as Creator, Holy Scripture insists always that He is not a de-personalized God, far away from us. The beautiful *Psalm 139* shows us God as an involved, energetic God forming, shaping us, knowing all of our thoughts.

> O Lord, Thou has searched me and known me. Thou knowest my sitting down and my rising, Thou understandest my thought afar off. . .Whither shall I go from Thy spirit? Or whither shall I flee from Thy presence? If I ascend up into heaven Thou art there. If I make my bed in hell, behold, Thou art there. If I take the wings of the morning and dwell in the uttermost parts of the sea, even there shall Thy hand lead me and Thy right hand shall hold me. . .I will praise Thee; for I am fearfully and wonderfully made. Marvelous are Thy works and that my soul knows right well. . .Search me, O God, and know my heart. Try me and know my thoughts. And see if there be any wicked way in me and lead me in the way everlasting (Ps. 139: 1–3, 7–10, 14, 23–24).

God is not far from any of us. St. Paul preached to the Athenians and still preaches to us: "For in Him we live and move and have our being" (Acts: 17:28). The Old Testament is full of examples that show us God as not just an onmipotent Creator, but as a tender, loving Father. What beautiful images we find of God as a Father stooping down, embracing His people! "And in the wilderness where Thou hast seen how the Lord thy God bore thee, as a man bears his son in all the ways that you went until you came to this place" (Deut. 1:31).

God calls us forth and knows our name. Such tender love should remove fear from our hearts and replace it with boundless confidence and trust in Him.

I have redeemed Thee. I have called thee by thy name. Thou art mine. When thou passest through the water, I will be with thee and through the rivers, they shall not overflow thee. When thou walkest through the fire, thou shalt not be burned; neither shall the flame kindle upon thee. For I am the Lord thy God, the Holy One of Israel, thy Savior. . .Fear not; for I am with thee. . .Behold, I will do a new thing. Now it shall spring forth. Shall you not know it? I will even make a way in the wilderness and rivers in the desert (Is. 43: 1–3, 5, 19).

How can the modern prophet have any fear since the Father protects him "Does He not see my ways and count all my steps?" (Job 31:4). More than being merely powerful as a Father, the Heavenly Father in His perfections combines strength with tenderness. God the Father exceeds in His love for us the love of any human mother.

Can a woman forget her sucking child, that she should not have compassion on the son of her womb? Yes, they may forget; yet will I not forget thee (Is. 49:15).

Could the modern prophet have greater testimony that God is personally involved in our lives as our provident Father?

It is in the New Testament that the prophet hears the full revelation of God as our Father. Jesus makes it possible for us to experience that God is truly our Father by giving us this presence within. We are not to fear, not to be over-anxious or solicitous about what we are to eat or drink or put on (Lk. 12:22–31). For our Father, Jesus tells us, loves us and knows that we have need of such things. We must put Him first because that is truth. God is the Source of our life. We must seek the Kingdom of Heaven and all these other things will be added.

I know of a married man and woman led deeply into the Gospel radicalness by having been baptized in the Holy Spirit who literally sought the Kingdom of Heaven by

devoting all of their time to God's service. The husband
gave up his good paying job as an engineer. The church
where they lead the charismatic prayer community has a
box in the rear with a sign: "For Jack." This family with
seven children has never wanted in their child-like trust in
God the Father's providential love. They took Jesus'
revelation in the Gospel to be literally true!

St. Paul points out to the prophet the presence of this
loving Father immersed in the whole world and continually energizing the material creation to bring His loving plan
into its fullness through Jesus Christ. The prophet sees
events in the unfolding history of mankind, especially the
concrete events that shape his life in their inner dimension.
While his un-Christian brother sees only the surface of such
events, the prophet sees "inside" the whole world through
the light of his faith, especially that of a loving Father.
"And we know that all things work together for good to
them that love God, to them who are the called according
to His purpose" (Rom. 8:28).

It isn't so much that the prophet discerns between
what God wills and what He permits to happen in his life.
The only important issue is to realize that God the Father
is faithful to the New Covenant. He will be inside of all
events exercising His fidelity and love for us. He is Yahweh
who goes before us and will protect us. The prophet
therefore knows there cannot be any event that happens to
him that cannot be an opening to meet God as Father.

How the world today needs such prophets who can
"see" inside of all events and point out God's loving
fidelity to all men. A prophet lives in the world, in the
midst of the same events that shape the lives of other men.
But through his union with Christ and His Spirit he is able
to discover meanings far beyond those interpretations

given by his brothers who do not "see." Prophets are those who offer a reason for living because they have seen and experienced for themselves the Fatherhood of God. And these are the peo le Michael Quoist says will save history.

Every moment is the "now" moment in which the prophet meets his Father, does His holy will with joy and complete abandonment. Christianity is this loving relationship with the Father. It is not a series of commands. It is a new life in the Spirit of Jesus who teaches us that we are now children of the Father. "Whosoever shall not receive the Kingdom of God as a little child he shall not enter therein" (Mk. 10:15). The Greek Fathers called this childlike confidence in the Heavenly Father *parrhesia*, not one virtue, but a way of life, a state of being before the Father that flows from the ontological new nature that Jesus Christ through His Spirit has wrought in the Christian through Baptism.

As the prophet lives each day in the childlike recognition of the Father's deep love relationship toward him, his love and dependence on the Father also deepens. The words of Philip become a constant prayer: "Lord, show us the Father and it suffices us" (Jn. 14:8).

As the prophet believes that Jesus is in the Father and the Father is in Jesus (Jn. 14:11), so he believes that They both abide in him with the Holy Spirit (Jn. 14:23). He dares to do the work of the Father because he believes in Him who promised that greater works than these he shall do (Jn. 14:12). Such a Christian has entered into true freedom of the Holy Spirit. He can do all things. Above all, he can live through the Spirit's love living within him a life befitting a child of so loving a Heavenly Father. His whole life becomes one with Jesus Christ in His Spirt of praise and worship of the almighty Heavenly Father.

11.

The Prophet Hears The Word Of God

"If you continue in My word, then are you My disciples indeed. And you shall know the truth and the truth shall make you free" (Jn. 8:31–32).

The Christian religion is built up on the faith in God's Word. When God spoke to Moses in the burning bush, he *heard* God reveal that He was *Yahweh*. Moses was curious; he wanted to approach closer; he desired to *see* God. But no one can approach God by seeing Him either with one's physical eyes, for "God is spirit" or with the eyes of the intellect. God speaks His Word and in the Word He communicates Himself to man.

In the Old Testament this Divine Word of God is not something abstract about which man reasons. It is primarily a fact of experience. The Prophets of the Old Testament experienced God's Word. They were conscious that God was speaking to them. His Word had a tremendous, revolutionizing effect in their lives. The Word comes into their lives and takes over as they surrender to its message, even at times at a violent cost to themselves (Amos 7:15; Jer. 20:7ss). Prophets knew they were in direct communication with the living God and they were receiving a message to be transmitted to the People of God. The people had a responsibility to recognize God's message in the words of the Prophets and to accept it so as to guide their lives by that message.

THE WORD OF GOD REVEALS

The Word of God in the Old as well as in the New
Testament is always a Word of revelation spoken to His
People. God reveals to man His will, the way man is to live
in order to please God. Moses received from God a plan of
life codified in the ten *Words*, the *Decalogue*, of God.
These were God's essential demands, the basics, upon
which God would further build His revelation. The Law of
Moses is received as the Word of God, giving man a way of
life pleasing to God. "Blessed are the undefiled in the way,
who walk in the law of the Lord. Blessed are they that
keep His testimony and that seek Him with the whole
heart" (Ps. 119:1–2).

The Word of God reveals not only God's will for man,
but reveals to him that God will be in His Word, acting to
accomplish His Word. God not only speaks His Word but
His Word is God's action in man's life, a force, a power,
God's infinite energies protecting His Chosen People. "I
am the Lord, thy God who have brought thee out of the
land of Egypt, out of the house of bondage" (Exod. 21, 2).

But the Word of God also unveils the future in
advance. A step at a time, this Word enlightens Israel, the
Prophets of old and the modern prophets today as to
God's plan. God is faithful to His promises, both in this
moment and in the fullness of time when His plan will be
completely fulfilled.

GOD ACTS THROUGH HIS WORD

The modern prophet is convinced from Holy Scripture and from his own experience that God's Word is a

living Word. God's revelation is not merely an intelligible message to man. It is a dynamic power which accompanies the message and which brings the message to its fullness God's Word goes forth and returns fulfilled. "He sent His word and healed them and delivered them from their destructions" (Ps. 107:20).

> So shall My word be that goes forth out of My mouth. It shall not return unto Me void, but it shall accomplish that which I please and it shall prosper in the thing whereto I sent it. For you shall go out with joy and be led forth with peace; the mountains and the hills shall break forth before you into singing and all the trees of the field shall clap their hands (Is. 55:11–12).

The prophet believes that when God reveals His Word, He will fulfill what He reveals in that Word. History is not outside of God's Word, but it is the unfolding of God's revealed Word. God first spoke His Word in creation and the world sprang into existence. His Word remains active in the universe, governing the stars (Is. 40:26) and everything of nature (Ps. 107:25).

Yet this Word of God is like a mighty two-edged sword. It is not always according to man's wisdom, the wisdom of God's revelation. It separates God's wisdom from any human, frail, sinful way of looking at man's history.

> For the word of God is quick and powerful and sharper than any two-edged sword, piercing even to the dividing asunder of soul and spirit and of the joints and marrow and is a discerner of the thoughts and intents of the heart (Heb. 4:12).

AND THE WORD WAS MADE FLESH

The Christian who eagerly listens to God's Word in Holy Scripture knows that God's Word in the Old Testament gradually became spoken by God so clearly that it finally assumed flesh in the Person of Jesus Christ. For the Christian of the New Covenant, Jesus Christ is the Word of God that contains all the words of God's former revelation. He is the fullness of the Father and in this living Word "All things were created by Him and for Him" (Col. 1:16).

> In the beginning was the Word and the Word was with God and the Word was God. The same was in the beginning with God. All things were made by Him and without Him was not anything made that was made. In Him was life and the life was the light of men. And the light shines in darkness; and the darkness comprehended it not (Jn. 1:1–5).

His every word flows from the Word of God and is a power. With a word Jesus silences the stormy waters and turns water into wine. The power of His words that effect miracles are signs of the Kingdom of God (Matt. 8:8). With a word He shows His power to change hearts, making men to become children of God by the will of God (Jn. 1:13). He speaks a word and bestows that same power upon His disciples (Matt. 18:18).

Jesus speaks the words of God (Jn. 4, 34). He speaks what the Father has taught Him (Jn. 8:28). His words are "spirit and life" (Jn. 6:63). Whoever abides in His words will be His disciple and he shall know the truth and the truth shall make him free (Jn. 8:31–32). Jesus does not speak of Himself, but only "as the Father said unto Me, so I speak" (Jn. 12:50). The prophetic Word found in the Old Testament finds in Him its perfect fulfillment.

MAN'S RESPONSE TO THE WORD

Although God speaks to us through His Word, Jesus Christ, it is up to us to let this Word be heard in our lives. How clearly Jesus Christ taught in the parable of the sower who went out to sow some seed the various responses of human beings to God's Word. Some seed fell by the wayside and was devoured by the birds. Some fell upon rocky soil and could not sink deep roots into rich soil and so the shoots soon withered. Some fell among thorns which choked the new life from the seeds. Others fell upon good ground and brought forth various degrees of fruit. It is Jesus Christ, God's Word, who gives us the inspired exegesis with His own inner meaning. There is an influence from Satan preventing us from receiving the Word into our hearts. There are the cares of this world, the desires for worldly riches that suffocate the new life from the seed. But who receives the Word of God and brings forth fruit abundantly is the one who hears the Word and *understands* it.

Again Jesus gives us men's responses to Himself, God's Word, by describing the one who *hears* His Word and puts it into practice against the one who hears the Word and does not live it (Matt. 7:24–26; Lk. 6:47–49). It is similar to a man who builds his house on rock or on sand. Each man will be judged by his attitude before the Word. For the Christian the Word is always being spoken in his heart. His response measures what choice he makes toward the Word, but this choice influences him for all eternity. Only those who listen to the Word and remain in it will have eternal life and will never see death (Jn. 8:51). Many Christians find the Word of God too demanding and walk away, but they move out of light back into darkness.

THE PREACHED WORD OF GOD

When the Word of God was muffled on Calvary and extinguished so that there was only darkness and silence over the earth, God marvelously "by the game of the Resurrection," to use the phrase of Teilhard de Chardin, continues to speak to men His Word. This does not primarily mean the words of Jesus Christ collected and repeated by His disciples but rather it is the very message of the Gospel proclaimed in the Church's *kerygma* or preached Word. It is a service of the Word preached to all nations boldly. It is the "Word of Salvation" (Acts 13:26); the "Word of Life" (Phil. 2:16), the living and efficacious Word (Heb. 4:12).

That preached Word has been written down, especially in the New Testament writings so that the Bible is more than a collection of Jesus Christ's words and deeds. In a very real way the Bible is the Word of God, Jesus Christ. Our contact with Jesus Christ is through this written, prophetic Word. That is why it is a living Word! It has a personality. God's Word is still among us speaking to us at each moment.

The modern prophet loves Holy Scripture because it is God's Word. The first Christians had the same understanding. As the message of Jesus Christ was preached, His Word grew. The Body of Christ was the Christian community receiving God's Word, Jesus Christ, into their lives and allowing Him to increase in them. That is why St. Luke could write in the *Acts*: "So mightily grew the Word of God and prevailed" (Acts 19:20).

In the Byzantine Liturgy each day the Gospel is carried in solemn procession by the deacon or priest among the people. Then he stands in front of the people and shouts out: "Wisdom! Let us be attentive!" All the people bow down to the Book as to Jesus Christ Himself. This same conviction was enacted each day during the Vatican Council II when each session in St. Peter's Basilica was begun with a solemn enthronement of the Gospel. The Word of God in Holy Scripture is Jesus Christ! He dwells among us still through this written Word. But it is a living Word, with God's fresh message, one with the very message that Jesus preached during his earthly existence and yet always freshly new.

The modern prophet knows the power of the Word of God for he knows it is Jesus Christ Himself. He eagerly is nourished by his prayerful study and preaching of God's Word in Holy Scripture. "Thy words were found and I did eat them. Thy words were unto me a joy and rejoicing of my heart" (Jer. 15:16). With Job he can say: "I have treasured up the words of His mouth more than my necessary food" (Job 23:12).

What wonders does God work through the modern prophet who takes the Word of God in Holy Scripture seriously! He takes that Word as really present to him as the Word made flesh was to His disciples and the spoken word preached by the disciples to the early Church before that Word became a written Word. He hears Jesus Christ clearly saying to him through Holy Scripture: "Lo, I am with you always, even unto the end of the world" (Matt. 28:20). It is God's *new* Word being communicated to the modern prophet.

Praying over the words of Holy Scripture gives birth in the heart of the Christian to deeper faith, hope and love. The Spirit of Jesus gives him understanding and knowledge of the Word. St. Paul prayed the prayer of all prophets as they approach Holy Scripture: "That I may know Him and the power of His resurrection and the fellowship of His sufferings, being made comformable unto His death" (Phil. 3:10).

Jesus Christ is alive and seen in His living Word. Thus the modern prophet eagerly opens Scripture to be with God's Word, Jesus Christ. It is no longer a dry study of Scripture but it is a heart-to-heart encounter with Jesus Christ, "the same yesterday, today and always" (Heb. 12:8). That same Word speaks to him of the Father's infinite, tender love for him. The same Jesus Christ is not only promising to send the Paraclete but actually is releasing Him anew as "living waters" from within.

The prophet today yields to the authority of the Word of God, to His healing power and wisdom. He finds God's enlightenment and direction concerning his daily problems in that Word.

The prophet not only has the living Word of God in his heart but also on his lips. It becomes "bone of his bone," spirit in his spirit. Such a prophet speaks the Word of God in his thoughts, conversation, in his every action and attitude manifested in social relations toward others.

Jesus Christ has come in the flesh and now in his gloriously resurrected presence lives still and gives Himself to all who open themselves to the Word of God. The prophets of old proclaimed the Word of God. It was the same Word Himself who would take flesh and speak God's revelation directly in human words to modern man.

Today as always since His coming in the flesh, man's problem is one of recognizing God's Word made flesh, Jesus Christ, in the Word that God is always speaking to men. Who does not hear that Word remains in darkness and is judged by that very fact (Jn. 3; 17ss). But to the many modern prophets who hear that living Word, God frees them from themselves, from the worldly values surrounding him and from sin and death to become a channel of grace for others. God speaks His Word through the humanity of Jesus Christ. But the humanity of Jesus Christ, gloriously risen, is extended into our world and time, into this present moment by speaking His Word, in continuity with the written Word in Holy Scripture, in the hearts of purified modern prophets who are willing to hear that Word and let it take complete control over their lives. Only one who has truly heard that Word can give that Word as health and life to the world. Mary, the Mother of that Word made flesh, is the model in her virginal listening and surrendering of self to that Word in order that she may then mother that same Word for others. "Behold the handmaid of the Lord; be it unto me according to thy word" (Lk. 1:38).

12

The Prophet Discerns

"Wherefore be not unwise, but understanding what the will of the Lord is" (Eph. 5:17).

The secret of a happy and successful Christian life is to do each thought, word and deed out of love for God. It is to seek always as Jesus Christ did in His earthly life to please His Heavenly Father in all things. Love is proved by deeds but not just any deeds. The deeds that please God are deeds accomplished according to His holy will. The deeds are important as signs of our submission totally in love to please Him. If we love another, we must want to please that person in all things best for that person. Jesus tells us: "If you keep My commandments, you shall abide in My love. Even as I have kept My Father's commandments and abide in His love" (Jn. 15:10).

In His earthly life Jesus strove always to keep the commandments of the Heavenly Father. ". . .not My will, but Thine be done" (Lk. 22:42). It is clear that many areas of His life were clearly seen by Him as commands of the Father. Cost Him personally whatever price, even His own life, He obeyed what He saw as the clear manifestation of the will of His Father in the commands given Him to fulfill. Surely His agony in the Garden and death on the Cross show us that Jesus regarded dying on the Cross for the sins of the world as a clear command of the Father.

Also in His life there were whole areas of decisions that seem to have been made very spontaneously, sometimes with reflection, sometimes in deep, silent prayer. Here we see a more delicate discernment of the will of His loving Father. This embraces the whole area of His seeking not merely to do the commands of the Father but in all things to seek to do the slightest wish. A command is different from a wish even though both come from the same person that we love. It requires greater love, delicacy and discernment to ask what is the wish of the Father in this or that circumstance of the life of Jesus than merely to fulfill His commands. For this He moved under the power of the Spirit in greater submission and surrender.

But lastly there are areas in the Gospel stories wherein a still higher degree of return of love for love are indicated. Besides seeking always to do the commands of the Father and to do His slightest wish made known through His Spirit of Love, Jesus Christ, who had experienced in His humanity the love of the Father as no other person on the face of the earth had, sought to please His Father.

> And He that sent Me is with Me. The Father has not left Me alone. For I do always those things that please Him (Jn. 8:29).

This is the highest degree of human freedom and requires the greatest delicacy to judge that what one wants to do for God is really in accord with His other commands and His habitual wishes. Yet here we find no indication of a "must." It is not a question of obligation for the Father does not express His will one way or the other. This is in the area of utter spontaneity where Jesus seeks to "improvise" ways to "flesh" out in human terms His return of love for the infinite love He has experienced from the Father toward Him. As the Father's love is an outpouring of total self-giving to His Son, it partakes of a *kenosis*, an emptying.

Much in the supreme giving of Himself to the Father in the Passion and terrifying emptying of Jesus on the Cross is explained only by an understanding of the dynamics of folly of the Cross in terms of wanting to give and give until there is nothing more to give. The unworldly spirit of self-seeking or of obedience to God's commands under pain of eternal punishment cannot understand the awful self-emptying of Jesus in His Passion and death. Is it too far-fetched to believe that His acceptance of so much pain and humiliation, abuse and rejection during His Passion was because the Father had decreed every detail? The Father asked Him to die for mankind on the Cross. Many of the terrifying details of that emptying, even to the last drop of blood and water, until there was nothing held back, have a greater meaning when we understand them in the dynamics of Jesus' overwhelming love for the Father. He had received an infinite, "kenotic" love of the Father who poured Himself out totally into the Son. The Father, out of the sheer folly of His own perfection as Love itself, wanted to give totally with nothing of the Fatherhood held back that He did not wish to share with the Son. So Jesus desired to empty Himself in a similar manner of love for love. Yet He had a body to act out this desire.

Hence "creative suffering" for Jesus was no obligation; it was not even wished by the Father. But He freely, spontaneously improvised ways to act out His surrender in perfect love back to the Father for the perfect love He had received from Him, the Source of His Being. St. John who stood at the foot of the Cross delicately adds the detail years later when he compiled his Gospel that, when Jesus Christ thirsted with a maddening thirst that raged through His body and the soldiers offered Him some vinegar and myrrh that would deaden somewhat the pain, Jesus allowed it to be touched to His lips but would not take it (Jn. 19:28–30).

Many of the humiliations during His trials He bore meekly as He emptied Himself still more of His control over His life to surrender more completely in love to the Father. Only one who has deeply loved can understand how one, not in a sickly masochistic way, but in the healthiest human way, can actually accept and seek sufferings, more and more, in order that his love for God can grow more intensely. This is always in proportion to the degree of love experienced from God. Hence one, not experiencing such flaming love of God, will always "discern" such suffering as wasted pain. St. Paul rejoiced in his sufferings for he wanted to be crucified with Christ Jesus, bearing in his body the marks of His Passion. "That I may know Him and the power of His resurrection and the fellowship of His sufferings, being made conformable unto His death" (Phil. 3:10).

St. Ignatius of Antioch wrote to the Romans at the beginning of the second century before he died for Christ in the amphitheater in Rome that he wanted to be ground by the teeth of the raging lions like wheat is ground into flour to become the Body of Jesus Christ. It was he who said it for all true Christians who through the love of the Holy Spirit understand that "Now that I suffer I become a Christian."

We see, therefore, that the term "to do the will of God" admits of several degrees. The crucial question is how to know that we are truly doing what falls under the will of God. The spiritual gift of discernment bestows upon the modern prophet a supernatural ability to discern the commands, the wishes and the complacency of God in regard to his own life and in regard to the lives of other individuals as well as the life of a total Church or nation or world.

The modern prophet must be concerned just as the Prophets of old with the discerning for his nation of the mind of God. He has a message through his work and daily contacts in the world to recall his brothers to the basic principles of Christian life and action. Such a prophet brings the message of God from the Church to the arena of the world: the factory, the office, the construction site and the kitchen. In this prophetic role, the prophet must be able to discern the commands of God, the wishes of God and what would most please the Father in the times and events of today. To do this, the prophet must grow in discernment.

Scripture shows us that God reveals His mind in many different ways. God spoke His commands through Moses and the ten commandments given for His people, Israel. He declared His wishes for His people through the Prophets who delicately listened to His inspirations. St. Joseph was told in a dream that he should take Mary and the child Jesus into Egypt and after the death of Herod He instructed him in another dream to return in safety to Palestine. Peter was given a vision of God's plan for the redemption of the Gentiles. Paul and Barnabas were selected to preach to the Gentiles by the Church of Antioch through prayer and fasting that allowed them to hear the Holy Spirit. "As they ministered to the Lord and fasted, the Holy Spirit said, 'Separate me Barnabas and Saul for the work whereunto I have called them' " (Acts 13:2).

In these and many other such ways God has unfolded

His will and purpose to mankind; He continues to do this even to the present time, The prophet is convinced that God has a plan for his life and for that of every other human being, for his nation and for the whole world. He believes that through one method or another, God will communicate His mind to man. Holy Scripture assures him repeatedly that he need not stumble through life in a confused and bewildered way. God is supreme intelligence; He is more willing to manifest to men His intentions and what would most please Him than any individual man is willing to know the mind of God.

Corrie Tee Boom has written so often in her books: "God has no problems, only plans!" With the Spirit of God comes a sense of truth, a sense of the way God works, an appreciation of God's values, what He commands, what He wishes, what would give Him great pleasure. The Spirit convicts us of sin (the values of the world) and truth and righteousness (Jn. 16:8).

The prophet knows that if he is to hear the Spirit in his life he must purify his heart. "Blessed are the pure of heart for they shall see God" (Matt. 5:8). He must die to sin in his life, to the false values of the world, the flesh and the devil. Prayer and fasting, moderation in controlling his appetites for food, sex, knowledge, etc. and control of all his thoughts are most important to overcome the fragmentation found within him preventing him from being truly open to the Holy Spirit.

TO KNOW GOD'S WILL

In his book: *How to Know God's Will*, Dr. Hobart E. Freeman points out that while God's purpose for every individual will vary inasmuch as no two individuals are alike in their needs, spiritual maturity, understanding, obedience or function in the Body of Christ, each Christian will find God's will the same for all in *three* basic areas.

After conversion, every Christian can be assured that God's will is that he receives the promise.

> And being assembled together with them, He commanded them that they should not depart from Jerusalem, but wait for the promise of the Father of whom, He says, you have heard from Me. For John truly baptized with water but you shall be baptized with the Holy Spirit not many days hence (Acts 1: 4–5).

Jesus promises us that the Spirit of God will come and dwell within us. He will empower us to live according to the will of God and do all things that please Him. If we are confused as to the mind of God, we can be assured of knowing that mind by accepting Jesus' promise that the Spirit is the "Spirit of truth" (Jn. 16:13). The fruit of the Spirit is "love, peace and joy. . ." (Gal. 5:22). If we have peace and joy it will be because out of our great love towards so loving a Heavenly Father we are not only seeking but knowing and accomplishing through the Holy Spirit all His commands, wishes and are striving to please Him in all things that render us imitators of Jesus Christ.

Jesus therefore promises us the continued presence and guidance of the Holy Spirit. The modern prophet has therefore a new vision as he yields himself up to the Spirit. He becomes delivered from his own selfish views and errors and God leads him into wisdom and understanding concerning His will for every relationship in the prophet's life.

> Wherefore be not unwise but understanding what the will of the Lord is. . .be filled with the Spirit (Eph. 5:17–18).

The Christian prophet is constantly aware of Jesus' promise that the Holy Spirit will teach him and remind him of everything He has ever told him (Jn. 14:26). He teaches others how to discern the will of God in their lives by a similar surrendering of oneself completely to the power of the Spirit.

CRUCIFIED WITH CHRIST

The second area of obligation for all who strive to know the will of God is to accept the crucified life with Christ that we may experience the fullness of Christ. As in the earthly life of Christ there are today many ready to follow Him in power, miracles, fame but there are few ready to follow a crucified Savior. The Spirit will take over in our lives illuminating us at each step as to the mind of the Father only if we hollow out of our lives any resistance to Christ "that you may be filled with all the fullness of God" (Eph. 3:19).

St. Paul puts it simply in terms of being crucified with Christ so that he no longer lives himself but Christ lives totally in dominance.

> I am crucified with Christ. Nevertheless, I live, not I, but Christ lives in me. And the life which I now live in the flesh I live by the faith of the Son of God who loved me and gave Himself up for me (Gal. 2:20).

The prophet bears the wounds of Christ's Passion within himself and witnesses to the need of all Christians to follow Christ suffering. "If any man will come after Me, let him deny himself and take up his cross and follow Me" (Matt. 16:24). There can be no true discerning the will of God except through a dying process, a readiness to be totally open to do not our own wills but solely the will of God. He can shout His command, He can whisper delicately His wish, the Spirit can urge us in charity to imitate the emptying of the Son for the Father, it makes little difference for the prophet who sees all three as manifestations of the one great desire in his life: will this please my Heavenly Father?

This stage is not so much concerned with what God is asking of us. It touches more the area of our total surrender of our lives to God and this is a death, a process of continued shouldering of the cross. It is a process of yielding to the Spirit promptly without resistance. To "let go" of our lives is to let the grain of wheat fall into the earth and die to bring forth the wonderful fruit of pleasing always the Father (Jn. 12:24).

God loves a broken, contrite heart and this brokenness can come about only through relinquishing our own wills. This spells suffering and the cross as a constant element in our lives.

Part of this continued suffering in the life of the prophet comes from his belief that God is supreme in his life and he puts his total trust in Him in each event while he tends to distrust his own interests unless they first tally with the values of God.

CONFESS THE LORD

The third area of obligation on all Christians seeking to do God's will is to confess that He is Lord and to wish only to be guided by Him. In the ultimate analysis, if the other two preceding elements are present, the final one is the directing force that purifies our intention and keeps us

always "sincere." Sincerity or honesty before the Lord, if ·
true, is about all we can really give to God; it is the
element in love that makes love a true surrender of
ourselves to God. If this is missing, we may have much
suffering in our lives and may be very open to receive the
fullness of the Spirit's power but rapine will have been
introduced into the holocaust. Good seed was planted but
an enemy sowed also weeds.

Thus the actual discovering of the will of God may
come about in many ways such as in reading the Word of
God, in prayer, by direct or indirect revelation, but the
ultimate element is to discern that the mind of God has
been manifested to us through the Holy Spirit.

We can hear this voice of the Spirit in many ways. It
is important that we do not force the Spirit to speak to us
in only one way. Often Christians say: "I will know it is
the will of God if tomorrow God appears to me in a
vision." Other signs might be selected by us, forcing God
to meet our terms or else we simply will not believe that
He has spoken. We feel smug and important. "If God really
loves me, He ought to speak to me clearly so that I will
really know His will. Knowing that, of course, I will do it.
But I won't act until I am sure!"

We cannot force God to meet our conditions and still
believe we are surrendering ourselves to His Spirit and
embracing the cross of suffering through total faith and
distrust in ourselves! This is evidently a bad spirit within
us, the spirit not of faith and trust but of pride and
ultimately of blasphemy against God as though He really
were not the Supreme Being in our lives but that He needs
to accommodate Himself to us.

But God does sometimes reveal His mind in strong
assurances through a revelation received in vision or

prophecy as happened in the conversion of St. Paul. But usually God works much more simply, demanding more faith and greater sincerity on our part. We must believe that the Spirit speaks to us in the Word and in prayer and as we grow in delicacy to His voice, we gain more in discernment. The Spirit makes it possible that our inner spirit is assured that what is given to do, to accept as true, to correct in us as false, is of the Holy Spirit. Often we add to the inner attraction given us by the Spirit towards some action to be done through reflecting on such with our reasoning powers. We see how this action fits into God's general plan of our life, how it tallies with His values as manifested in Holy Scripture and the lives of the saints. We can then consent to the inspiration and embrace it with peace and joy. The peace and joy that follow such a decision or leading of the Spirit are good indications that the whole process has been under His leadership. If a decision ends up with great turmoil and bitter feelings, a lack of peace and diminishment of love within us, we can readily suspect a bad spirit at work.

We must be cautious of the word "feeling." Sometimes the Spirit speaks to us to do something most difficult. There can be a feeling of resentment, fear of our own powers to succeed; yet overall there will be a deeply rooted feeling of assurance and peace that this is what the Spirit is asking. Mere emotion can easily be rooted in self-centeredness. This inner intuition or attraction that the Spirit is leading us under His power is beyond how we feel. Peace is a fruit of the Spirit that pervades our whole being. A "feeling" is rooted usually in an automatic reaction that usually flows from our sinful situation that has remained unhealed by the Savior.

THE SPIRIT SPEAKS IN MANY WAYS

As the prophet learns to listen to the inner voice of the Holy Spirit speak to him, he opens himself to His words constantly in a freedom that surprises him in the variety of ways that the Spirit will speak. One common way He speaks to the prophet is by prophecy. This can be both as a prophecy given him in prayer or as he ministers to others, for himself or for others, individually or as a Church or a nation, by way of exhortation, admonishment or foretelling the future.

It can be the Spirit's voice that comes through an anointed teaching, again given the prophet directly as he teaches or studies or indirectly from another teacher anointed with a message. This can be a very frequent manner in which the Spirit speaks to Spirit-filled Christians today.

Often the Spirit speaks through our ordinary circumstances of life. People near us, seemingly dropping a word, a suggestion, recounting an incident, even a dream, can prepare us to hear the Spirit. Here one tends more to weigh what is of the Spirit from the ordinary human event by seeing that the new message does not contradict God's previous workings. This refers mainly to the full performance of our normal duties of the state of life in which God has placed us.

The prophet of today must step out of the ranks of the pampered Christians and learn to rely entirely on God for all his needs. Most of us shudder at the idea of trusting in anything but medicare, insurance policies, etc. The prophet learns to live a life of childlike faith, fully trusting in God for all his needs. It is a delicate line between trusting in God to meet our needs and trusting in God recklessly and doing nothing that God's own will would want us to do. Discernment is open to all ways in which God wishes to reveal His will to the prophet. But his beginning point of trust is completely in God's fidelity that He will communicate His mind to man. "I will say of the Lord: He is my refuge and my fortress. My God in Him will I trust" (Ps. 91:2).

God will not fail him in any of the promises He has made.

> God is not a man, that He should lie. Neither has the son of man, that he should repent. Shall He not do what He has said? Shall He not make good what He has spoken? (Num. 23:19).

The prophet learns to lean on God above all. He does not lean upon his own understanding alone. This does not mean that he does not use his intelligence and reasoning powers that God gave him. It is a matter of letting God speak through any and all means including man's own reasoning over a situation. The prophet first learns the truth of *Proverb's* statement: "In all thy ways acknowledge Him" (Prov. 3:6). By confessing God to be the source of all knowledge, man can use his own intelligence to discern God's ways, but it is primarily God alone that the prophet is interested in hearing. Thus the prophet discerns God's will by professing at all times God's goodness, love, guidance and protection of man at all times. He believes that if he asks God, He will grant his petition. If he asks to know God's will, God will speak and give him the assurance in faith that what he concludes to be God's attraction will be the source of pleasing the Heavenly Father. Discernment is the sensitivity that is given to those who love the Lord with all their hearts to hear God's voice tell them what will most please Him. It is tied to love!

13

The Prophet Mediates

"And for this cause He is the Mediator of the New Testament" (Heb. 9:15).

Every city has its "gehenna," a place on its outskirts, hidden from the eyes of most of its inhabitants, where the unwanted "junk" and garbage that accumulate in a city can be burned and disposed of. In the Pacific Ocean society had heaped its undesirables, its uncleaned lepers onto the island of Molokai.

One day a missionary priest came there dragging a case with all that he owned. He was saying that he came to help these lepers. But it was only 15 years later, when on a Sunday Father Damian rose before his congregation of lepers and addressed them as "Fellow lepers!" that he won their confidence. He was finally one of them. He too had leprosy. Now he could touch them, help them, be their mediator before God. They knew now he loved them and sought only to help them.

One of the most heart-gnawing experiences common to all human beings is that of loneliness. We all know what it means to feel isolated from everyone. There seems at times to be no one who understands us. No one to smile at us, give us a pat on the back, look lovingly into our eyes and assure us of their unselfish love and devotion. When we project this feeling of loneliness and estrangement to the whole human race, we begin to understand a bit better what it meant in God's designs that Jesus Christ, the Word of God made flesh out of love for us, should empty Himself of all dignity to take upon Himself the form of a servant (Phil. 2:6–8) to win our trust.

> He was wounded for our transgressions. He was bruised for our iniquities. The chastisement of our peace was upon him and with his stripes we are healed (Is. 53:5).

He became sin for our sakes that we might be delivered from sin. St. Peter powerfully describes Christ's infinite love for mankind: "Who His own self bore our sins in His own body on the tree that we, being dead to sins, should live unto righteousness, by whose stripes you were healed" (1 Pet. 2:24). Jesus Christ, being God, always merited to stand before His Heavenly Father, to intercede with Him for the whole world with infinite dignity and power. Yet His mediation for mankind had to be first a winning of man's trust in Him. He was by nature the mediator of the Father. All things were created in and through Him.

Yet to qualify to become the mediator of man, to be the spanning bridge over into humanity, He had to dip into the other side, to be rooted in the bank of humanity as He was from all eternity by nature rooted in the bank of divinity. Man's alienation from God through sin caused an abyss of loneliness within his heart that could not be alleviated except by an experience of love at first hand. In the fullness of time, God became man, "the Word became flesh and dwelt among us" (Jn. 1:14). "For God sent not His Son into the world to condemn the world, but that the world through Him might be saved" (Jn. 3:17).

The beginning of redemption is the moving out of my

loneliness by an experience that God really loves me to the folly of the Cross and that, as St. Paul would say so often, "For me He died!" Jesus Christ therefore becomes the greatest of all prophets because He literally stands between God and man and through the love of His Holy Spirit He goes to the Father in perfect, self-surrendering love while at the same time He goes toward each human being in that same perfect, self-giving love. Jesus Christ therefore mediates man to God not so much by words said but by a presence of self-surrendering love.

The prophet today is primarily this type of mediator. We know that there is only one, unique Mediator and that is Jesus Christ. He has replaced all other mediators such as Moses and the early prophets, all other sacrifices of the Temple unto blood of animals. He is the Mediator who can reconcile the two separated parties, God and the human race, because He belongs to both worlds. He is God and Man. He is the only ultimate High-Priest because He, the Offerer, is also the Gift Offered. He is the Priest and the gift offered at the same time.

> And for this cause He is the mediator of the New Testament, that by means of death, for the redemption of the transgressions that were under the first Testament, they who are called might receive the promise of eternal inheritance (Heb. 9:15).

Yet the prophet by participating through the power of the Holy Spirit as intimately as possible with the sufferings of the human race, its sinfulness and alienation from God, seeks also by deep, prayerful union to abide in Jesus Christ and through His powerful intercession to beg the Father for forgiveness and reconciliation. The Prophet Jeremiah is a very special model of a prophet mediating. No other prophet shows his intense feeling and compassion for the fate of his people. He associates with their infidelity, pleads before God with confidence, is torn asunder by the coldness and rejection of him and of God's covenant by his own people.

Jeremiah becomes a model of Jesus Christ and of the modern prophet through his mediating God's message of conversion by his own example. We know how the kings had been chosen by God as mediators of His people. The king of Israel through his anointing became officially the representative of his people, the one to speak to Yahweh on behalf of the Chosen People. He rendered thanks to God for his people. He spoke lamentations in times of national crises. As he functioned on behalf of God's People, he was obligated to function also as God as far as possible by ruling the people with justice.

The prophets from the 8th century on replaced the kings and they mediated God's mercy toward a people that was turning away from God. Jeremiah brings in his own life the fullness of prophetic mediation as he becomes a model of what Jesus Christ would be toward God's new people.

Jeremiah pleads with God even though he feels it is hopeless. He, the prophet, the mediator, and his people become one and the same person. Yet he is also one with Yahweh. He understands why God should not renew His covenant with them. "You walk, every one of you, in the hardness of your evil heart" (Jer. 16:12). His heart is torn by his people's coldness to Yahweh. "Cleanse your heart of evil, O Jerusalem, that you may be saved" (Jer. 4:14). Yet he stands with boldness before Yahweh, never forgetting his people. He is aware of being called by God, even from the womb, to be dedicated to this mission of mediation of God and His people. Though he would like to run away from his calling, yet he continues in faith to stand before Yahweh and intercede.

And God heaps upon Jeremiah as upon a microcosm of Israel His wrath to the point of breaking him. Yet in faith he mediates his people by being totally obedient to Yahweh. God has His complete way with Jeremiah until Jeremiah is cut off completely from his people, rejected, alone: "Know that for Thy sake I have suffered rebuke. . .I sat not in the assembly of the mockers, nor rejoiced. I sat alone because of Thy hand, for Thou hast filled me with indignation" (Jer. 15:15–17).

The prophet is called to "aloneness," to stand between God and his people. Out of his great love for his people that has forgotten God he shares in their alienation from God. Although he loves God and seeks at each moment to do God's will, yet his love for his fellow-man becomes so great that he associates his sins with his own, as though he were the guilty one. With Moses he stands before the face of God and prays boldly that if God does not forgive the sin of his people "blot me, I pray Thee, out of Thy book which Thou hast written" (Exod. 32:32).

LOVE OF NEIGHBOR

So great is the love of the modern prophet for his people that he pleads in prayer that God may grant him to suffer for their punishment. St. Symeon the New Theologian (+1022) grasped the role of prophet as mediator and intercessor for his people in writing the following words:

> . . .he would wish with such zeal the salvation of his brothers, that often he would beg God, the Lover of men, with all his soul, with burning tears either to save them with him or to condemn him with them, refusing absolutely to be saved alone and in this imitating the attitude of God and that of Moses. So greatly tied spiritually to them by holy charity in the Holy Spirit, he would not even wish to enter into the Kingdom of Heaven if he had to be separated from them.

Like Jesus Christ, the modern prophet lives in two regions: he lives totally among men, feeling every tear, every suffering and anguish of his brother as his own. Yet he moves through life as though he were already in the presence of his Heavenly Father. He experiences daily that he is already a son of God and co-heir with Jesus Christ of Heaven forever (Rom. 8:17).

Today's prophet acts much as a chemical catalyst. He begins a process of internal action, of conversion of the heart. For this he must be completely within the process. Yet he must not become immersed in the process so that he is swept into the process and becomes something different than a mediator. A catalyst is not changed into the mass around him. He is a force to change the mass.

Paradoxically the modern prophet, as all God's prophets in the past, becomes a catalyst and mediator of His holy Word through a similar catalystic process that goes on in his soul. Paul writes: "And *almost* all things are by the law purged with blood; and without shedding of blood there is no remission" (Heb. 9:22). There is a perfecting, a cleansing that comes by ministering the word of God. It is the perfecting of the saints to render them supple instruments under the Holy Spirit to become true mediators through whom the Word of God may be communicated to others.

God puts His hand on the prophet called to mediate the Word. He cleanses His chosen instrument not only in his body, but in his soul and spirit. Every thought is placed under God's scrutiny. It is God's living Word within the prophet that cleanses him.

> Having therefore, brethren, boldness to enter into the holiest by the blood of Jesus, by a new and living way, which He has consecrated for us through the veil, that is to say, His flesh;

and having a high priest over the house of God; let us draw near with a true heart in full assurance of faith, having our hearts sprinkled from an evil conscience and our bodies washed with pure water (Heb. 10:19—20).

This cleansing, pure water is the Word of God. Can a prophet mediate God's word before he has been completely "washed" in it? The Word washes out of the prophet all that is false doctrine, all that comes from himself and is not mediating God's Word. It is losing one's own identity and putting on the mind of Jesus Christ in all things. "If you continue in My word, then are you My disciples indeed. And you shall know the truth and the truth shall make you free" (Jn. 8:31—32). To remain in Christ, the Word, the prophet must be listening for His voice. To become a mediator, one has to have an open mind to learn more and more all the time about the riches of that Divine Word. Remaining in that Word means constantly to study and think and pray about what the Divine Word has said in Scripture and is saying in the prophet's life today. It is complete obedience to that Word, to all of His commandments. One contemplates the Word and it leads him to action. The greatest function of mediating the Word is to mirror the Word completely in one's life as though the life of the modern prophet were to be a lived Gospel story told in modern terms understandable by his contemporaries. Thus he mediates the Word of God by being completely under the Word at all times in all of his thoughts, words and actions.

THE PROPHET-PRIEST

We have already said that Jesus Christ alone is our High Priest. He came to die for our sins and, in the offering and sacrifice of Himself completely for us (Eph. 5:2), He removes our sinful condition before the Heavenly Father and makes it possible that we can now have "communion" as children with the Father. Jesus still is our High Priest before the Father now and forever: "Jesus, made a high priest forever after the order of Melchisedec" (Heb. 6:20).

Jesus Christ differs from all priests before Him in the Old Testament and after Him in the New Covenant. He is completely without sin. His sacrifice was made once and for all. He needs not to die for us again. But the amazing point of Jesus' priesthood is that the sacrifice He offers on our behalf is of Himself. He offers and is offered.

> For such a high priest became us, who is holy, harmless, undefiled, separate from sinners and made higher than the heavens, who needs not daily, as those high priests, to offer up sacrifice, first for His own sins and then for the people's; for this He did once, when He offered up Himself (Heb. 7:26–27).

Still Jesus Christ calls everyone baptized in the name of the Trinity to share in His one priesthood. That priesthood consists in offering up in union with Jesus Christ spiritual sacrifices acceptable to God.

> You also, as lively stones, are built up a spiritual house, a holy priesthood, to offer up spiritual sacrifices, acceptable to God by Jesus Christ...But you are a chosen generation, a royal priesthood, a holy nation, a peculiar people; that you should show forth the praises of Him who has called you out of darkness into His marvelous light (1 Pet. 2:5, 9).

Besides the cultic priest of Christianity, ordained to renew the sacrifice of Christ and to gather up the united sacrifices of the Church that assembles in Jesus Christ's name to mediate the mercy of the Father in the blood of His Son, each Christian is called upon by his Baptism to mediate the priesthood of Jesus Christ before the Father on his own behalf and that of his fellow-men.

He can participate in this priestly mediation to the degree that he has first allowed the priestly mediation of Jesus to have its full reconciling effects to come upon him and transform him according to the priestly heart of Christ. The clear lesson from the Prophets of the Old Testament is that they first became their message. As their message was very much concerned with reconciling a hard-hearted nation of people back to God, they first individually had to enter into that complete sacrifice of their heart to God. Jeremiah knew that he had to have a cleansed heart first if his people were to hear his message from God and turn, through repentence, back to God. True religion and a true share in the priestly function of reconciliation can come only through an interior conversion of the heart.

After Jeremiah experienced this in his own heart, he was able to obtain the mercy and forgiveness of God toward his people and announce to them God's response:

> Behold the days are coming, says the Lord, that I will make a new covenant with the house of Israel and with the house of Judah. . .But this shall be the covenant that I will make with the house of Israel. After those days, says the Lord, I will put my law in their inward parts and write it in their hearts. And I will be their God and they shall be My People (Jer. 31:31, 33).

Although the modern prophet knows Jesus Christ is alone the Mediator of the human race with the Heavenly Father, yet he knows through God's transforming grace what God has made of him. "And all things are of God who has reconciled us to Himself by Jesus Christ and has given to us the ministry of reconciliation" (2 Cor. 5:18). The prophet is called into the awesome redemptive work by the merits of Jesus Christ to reconcile the sinful world to God. Jesus Christ has worked a work of purification in him so he can triumphantly cry out with St. Paul:

> I am crucified with Christ; nevertheless I live; yet not I but Christ lives in me and the life which I now live in the flesh I live by the faith of the Son of God, who loved me and gave Himself for me (Gal. 2:20).

Jesus Christ shares His divine life with the modern prophet, living in him as the vine is the life-giving source to the living branch. He is the Head, human beings in whom Jesus lives are the body. They are totally new in Him and share in His power to intercede before the Throne of the Father. He "has raised us up together and made us sit together in heavenly places in Christ Jesus" (Eph. 2:6). We have been empowered to use His merits and His Name which is the only name whereby we shall be saved (Acts 4:12). It is His mediation, His intercession that the prophet shares as he groans in the Spirit of Jesus on behalf of a race of people that has forgotten God. Like Abraham he begs, not on his own merits, but because of God's goodness made known through Jesus Christ, that men and women, cities and nations, the sick and suffering, the mentally confused and disturbed be spared and be healed and be reconciled with God.

Today the world has desperate need for prophets who mediate Jesus Christ and His intercessory power before the Father's throne on behalf of the human race. Jesus Christ wants to share His power, His love, His wisdom with the world; yet He still mediates His priestly mediation through human beings in whom He can have absolute power and freedom to work as He wishes. Absolute oneness with Christ makes not the prophet a mediator distinct from Jesus Christ, but renders the mediation of Jesus Christ concretized again in human terms on this earth. As the prophet is crucified with Christ Jesus, has died with Him, is justified with Him, made alive by Him, so he is raised with Him and now seated with Him before the throne. All of man's mediation comes from Jesus Christ. He is nothing; Jesus is all. There is only the High-Priest, Jesus Christ. But the modern prophet, like St. John the Baptist, mediates Jesus Christ. He is constantly pointing out to others: There is the Lamb of God. It is He who takes away the sins of the world! He must increase. I must decrease. All glory be to the Lamb of God.

> Unto Him that loved us and washed us from our sins in His own blood and has made us kings and priests unto God and His Father. To Him be glory and dominion forever and ever. Amen. (Rev. 1:5–6).

14

The Prophet Lets Go

"Fear not, little flock; for it is your Father's good pleasure to give you the Kingdom" (Lk. 12:32)

The end of our lives is to live in the presence of God as Father and in union with Jesus Christ who sends us His Holy Spirit to adore the All-Holy God by a total adoring surrender to His loving will. The prophet goes into the desert to be stripped of himself and all that keeps him from this surrender to God. There is a unique quality of any desert. It soon levels man down to his creaturely size. It removes any sham, pretence, false sophistication. Man's life is reduced to the basics. His vision stretches farther into eternity. He understands his poverty and weakness. In his utter need he learns to "leave himself" and open totally to God's presence. As he experiences God's deep love, he learns to "let go" and give God complete rein in his life.

Love flows out of the trust we have towards another. And yet love also increases the trust we can give the one loved. The Christian experience is one of experiencing the personal, involving love of the Trinity in our lives, not only in the great moments but in each and every moment.

The Israelites knew that Yahweh was not so much a name to be pronounced but He was the Fullness of being that was to be encountered in the moment that was about to burst upon them. God was faithful to His covenant. He would prove Himself as the absolute Source of their existence, the answer to their needs, the goal of all their aspirations.

In the desert, Moses and his followers opened themselves at each moment to God's creative, protective love. They became the Chosen People when they let go of their idols that they had created of God and of themselves. They had to learn not to anticipate by their own power their own protection against enemies. God demanded, as man's response to His fidelity, total surrender. "My son, give Me thy heart and let thine eyes observe My ways" (Prov. 23:26).

Joshua, Moses' successor, and his subjects bound themselves by oath to seek always to do God's commands.

> And the king stood by a pillar and made a covenant before the Lord, to walk after the Lord and to keep His commandments and His testimonies and His statutes with all their heart and all their soul, to perform the words of this covenant that were written in this book. And all the people stood to the covenant (2 Kgs. 23:3).

The sign of true love is self-surrender so as to be totally at the disposition of the one loved. The prophet in the desert enters into a new vision of reality. He sees the loving hand of God everywhere. Faith strips the shell away from the experience of the moment to reveal God's loving, dynamic, energetic presence at the heart of matter. He knows God cannot be in any place but is *everywhere*. God cannot cease to be what He is by essence, namely, loving. Hence he believes in God's holiness that makes Him so perfect and transcendent that He is never solely in one place. He believes also that He is love and therefore present in every place, in each event at each moment.

Like a child that has been called by his name in the outpouring of his father's providential care, the prophet learns to see the loving hand of God in everything that touches him. No event is too insignificant or banal, too impossible to be the point of contacting this loving Father. He who numbers every hair on man's head, will He not also take care of all his needs? (Lk. 12:7).

The present moment is the only point of the prophet's life in which he can seek out and find what will please his Heavenly Father. The desert teaches him that the past is precisely that; it is past. If it still exerts a power it is only because it is also present now in this moment. The future is not yet here. So much can happen now to change what he would like the future to bring him. He cannot live in anything but the present moment in which to surrender in loving service to God.

J-P. de Caussade, in his classical work on *Self-Abandonment to Divine Providence*, coins the happy term of "the sacrament of the present moment." We know that sacraments are visible signs made up of material things and gestures along with words that lead the believers into not only what the signs signify but help the believers to open up to the encounter of Jesus Christ to effect what the signs signify. By an extension through our Christian faith, we can say in an analogous way God's presence is found in each event of each moment and He is effecting a sacramental self-giving to the Christian that results in a greater union between man and God.

In the sacrament of the Holy Eucharist the priest breathes over bread and wine and with the intention of Jesus Christ and the words of consecration within the context of the Divine Liturgy the signs of bread and wine become points of encountering Jesus Christ as our food and drink. The prophet in his desert through his purified faith has the gift of the Holy Spirit to see God hidden "inside" of each encounter with the creatures that each moment brings to him. He reverences and adores that presence. He surrenders himself to God's loving presence to let God do with him whatever He wishes in that present moment. The prophet gives up his own control over his life, his desires, his plans for the moment and in total abandonment he yields to God's activity in that moment.

His child-like faith assures him that there is no circumstance happening in his life that is outside of God's control. Each event becomes a point of opening oneself to God's action. Such a Christian of purified faith learns to relax in God's omnipresence in all events. He is filled with trust and peace and joy that no one can take away. No event can destroy this surrendering adoration to God's will as it manifests itself at each moment.

This will requires man's action at a given moment. The prophet divines from his God-given reason what the will of God is asking of him in the performance of his ordinary duties of his state in life. He opens himself up to the gentle whisperings of the Holy Spirit to inspire him to be up and about the Father's business by actions of the moment that lie somehow beyond the ordinary duties of his state of life yet that do not contradict and impede those duties. Here the prophet presents himself in discernment to what reason and the dictates of the Holy Spirit in love for others demand.

There are also the manifestations of God's will, as Teilhard de Chardin describes in *The Divine Milieu*, that can be classified as passive diminishments. Here the prophet divines the will of God through what happens to him in which he does not take the initiative but rather "receives" action from outside, from other persons, creatures, external events or simply the attrition that comes from being a finite, material being subject to headaches, body aches and bruises, old age and finally, the greatest passive diminishment of all, death.

Father Walter Ciszek, S.J. tells in his book, *With God in Russia*, how he spent 23 years in the U.S.S.R. Fifteen of these years were spent in harrowing experiences in prisons like the infamous Moscow prison of Lubiyanka and concentration labor camps in the frigid Vorkuta Arctic Zone. Yet what gave him the super-human strength to accept, even with joy, every suffering, anguish, desolation and loneliness was the deep realization that his Heavenly Father was to be found working somehow or other in each moment. He did not have to live 15 years of confinement. He had to live merely *today*. He had only to find the suffering countenance of his dying Savior in the gasping fellow-prisoner who lay next to him dying from hunger and cold. The mystery of evil was not solved by him. It was conquered by the love of the Holy Spirit poured into his soul to accept each moment with joyful abandonment to the Heavenly Father.

Abandonment in the desert is not resignation like a whipped dog before an over-powering master. It is not adequately expressed by terms such as a submissive will, one that accepts the will of God or acquiesces or conforms to God's designs. Abandonment connotes the whole being in loving movement toward God. St. Francis de Sales defines it: "To abandon one's soul and to forsake oneself signifies nothing more or less than to deprive oneself of one's own will in order to give it up to God."

Such a Christian is indeed approaching the essence of what it means to be God's prophet. Teilhard de Chardin calls this quality of abandonment "passionate indif-ference." It is not a limp, willy-nilly attitude or a sick insensibility or apathy of the coward that is afraid to assume a positive stand toward life. True prophetic abandonment flows from the experience of God's tender love toward the individual. It recognizes man's own blindness and sinfulness; hence his own inability to know what is best for his over-all happiness. It confesses that God is all-wise and all-knowing. But above all, God is all-loving even in moments of purification, pruning, suf-fering.

The prophet stands on the mountain above all the petty yearnings of his sinful nature. He is balanced, waiting for the "still, small voice" of God to whisper His holy will. Like Samuel in the temple he is begging God, "Speak; for Thy servant hears!" (1 Sam. 3:10). God can speak His word as He wishes. There is no inclination, no wanting to hear one word rather than another. The prophet is total receptivity. He is a clean sheet of paper upon which God can freely write His word. Pliant and flexible, he is, in the words of St. Francis de Sales, "like a ball of wax in the hands of God, ready to receive with equal welcome all the impression of His eternal good-pleasure. . .like an infant that has not yet the power to will or love anything."

JESUS REVEALS TO US THE FATHER

The modern prophet knows that there is no knowing the Father in true religious experience that will give us a childlike abandonment except through Jesus Christ. He comes on earth not only to teach us the loving care that the Heavenly Father has for each one of us but Jesus lives out in His own personal love at each moment this abandonment. He who was wrapt in the face-to-face vision of the Father's infinite loving care for His Son came to share with us these secrets closed to human beings who do not hear His Word.

"He that has seen Me has seen the Father" (Jn. 14:9). Jesus poured out His mercy and compassion on the suffering multitude. He healed all that came to Him and told us that His Father would do the same.

> Ask and it shall be given you. Seek and you shall find. Knock and it shall be opened unto you. For everyone that seeks finds and to him that knocks it shall be opened. If a son shall ask bread of any of you that is a father, will he give him a stone? Or if he ask a fish, will he for a fish give him a serpent? Or if he shall ask an egg will he offer him a scorpion? If you then being evil, know how to give good gifts unto your children, how much more shall your Heavenly Father give the Holy Spirit to them that ask Him? (Lk. 11:9–13).

Against the formal rules of man, at least the Pharisees' interpretation of God's law of the Sabbath, Jesus followed His loving heart to heal the sick on that day. He was truly the Good Shepherd who followed after the lost sheep and worked patiently to lead it back as He did with the Samaritan woman at the well of Jacob to the well of eternal Living Water. He incurred the wrath and hatred of the official church leaders of His time by healing and forgiving sinners. He never was too tired to heal and lead the sick and weary to new health and happiness. His Father was really a prodigal Father who poured Himself out in tender forgiving love to the wayward son. He was like the woman who lost the coin and lighted a candle to sweep until she found it. He rejoiced more over the one lost sheep that returned to the fold than for the 99 that had not strayed.

Jesus Christ not only taught us that God is our Father, but He makes it possible to live this son-Father relationship by incorporating us into His very own Sonship and sending us the Holy Spirit who convicts us that we are truly sons of this loving Father.

> You have received the Spirit of adoption whereby we cry, Abba, Father. The Spirit bears witness with our spirit that we are the children of God; and if children, then heirs, heirs of God and joint heirs with Christ; if so be that we suffer with Him, that we may be also glorified together (Rom. 8:15–17). And because you are sons, God has sent forth the Spirit of His Son into your hearts, crying, Abba, Father. Wherefore thou art no more a servant, but a son; and if a son, then an heir of God through Christ (Gal. 4:6).

Through the Holy Spirit the prophet in the desert believes firmly that he has a loving Heavenly Father who is concerned with every particular of his life. Nothing is too insignificant for the Father's concern. Nothing too great lies outside of His power. The prophet therefore believes in Jesus' words:

> He that believes in Me, the works that I do shall he do also; and greater works than these shall he do, because I go to My Father. And whatsoever you shall ask in My name, that will I do that the Father may be glorified in the Son. If you shall ask anything in My name, I will do it. (Jn. 14:12–14).

ABANDONMENT AND PERSEVERING PRAYER

The prophet learns from the Holy Spirit how to be a child trusting in the Father's goodness to answer all prayers and yet how to persevere in asking without losing heart. God will grant his prayer as Jesus has assured him.

He knows, too, that he does not know how to pray but the Holy Spirit intercedes for him (Rom. 8:26). The Spirit quickens his heart to know when to persevere in asking for a necessary gift and not to falter in fear of being disappointed. The prophet remembers the Lord's parable of the neighbor who awakens his friend and asks for some bread because of the arrival of a friend. Even if he does not want to rise to give the bread because of his friendship, he will do so because of the insistent importunity (Lk. 11:5–10).

Jesus teaches us, exhorts us to go to the Father with courage, even boldness, mingled with a childlike trust in His great love. He convicts us that this gives great pleasure to His Father. It was this constantly abiding faith that gained for many in the Gospel a healing. "Thy faith has saved thee; go in peace" (Lk. 7:50). He repels the woman of Canaan who asked Him to heal her daughter. He seemingly insults her, telling her that He came only to save the lost sheep of the house of Israel. It was not right to take the children's bread and give it to dogs. If anyone ever had reason to stop asking, it was she. Yet her beautiful humility and deep persistent faith touched His heart: "True, Lord, yet the dogs eat of the crumbs which fall from their masters' table." His answer to such trusting faith was to heal her daughter: "O woman, great is thy faith. Be it done unto thee even as thou wilt" (Matt. 15:26–28).

The prophet, abandoned to God's providence and still persevering in petition, hears the words of Jesus: "Therefore I say unto you, what things soever you desire when you pray, believe that you receive them and you shall have them" (Mk. 11:24). He lets it up to the wisdom of God when and how to manifest His answer to prayer. But he is firmly convinced that God will certainly, absolutely answer his prayer, for God assures him of this. He knows from experience that when he asks for health God gives him an increase in a spiritual healing that is more precious than the temporary physical healing. The modern prophet believes he may be in need of a better job. God leads him into a situation that grants what the prophet really was praying for, not this or that better job, but a bettering of his whole life.

He learns that his trust in God to provide for all of his needs extends to all details of his life. Jesus taught this so strongly in order that the Christian child of God could be freed from undue preoccupations with such material concerns. The Father takes care of the grass, the trees, the flowers of the fields, the birds of the air. They have all they need. How much more, if the modern prophet will abandon himself to the loving care of the Father, will he not experience this Fatherly concern for all of his material needs? (Lk. 12:22–32).

The desert has brought the prophet into new awareness of his deeper spiritual needs. As God purifies him from his "managerial" hold over his life, the prophet experiences the dark night of the desert. A steel wall of darkness seems to confront him. God seems so absent. He feels his own sinfulness in isolation. He cries out a piercing cry into the long night that God come to his rescue. "My God, my God, why hast Thou forsaken me!" He feels that he will never look upon the loving face of his Father again. He does not despair but deepens his faith, his hope, his love. St. Bernard says: "Only he who has experienced it can believe what the love of Jesus is."

God will not leave the prophet; of this he is sure. The very hairs of his head are all numbered and of concern to his Father (Matt. 10:29–30). O God, come to my rescue, the prophet cries. And in a new way of experiencing God in darkness the prophet is at peace. The Father becomes more the Father as the son loves Him for·Himself and not merely for His consolations.

In all of the prophet's spiritual needs he turns with confidence to the Father in loving abandonment. He lovingly kisses His hand in all circumstances. He gives up any and all of his own plans for salvation. God alone is the Master, the Divine Potter who moulds as He wishes. The prophet begins to live fully on all levels for his deepening faith leads him to find God's loving presence and creative energies at work in each event, in each creature that he confronts. Everything is gift. All is received with praise and blessing to the Father of all good gifts that come down from above, the Father of lights (James 1:17). He is convinced by the inner knowledge that the Holy Spirit gives him that all things really do work unto good to those who love the Lord (Rom. 8:28).

The abandoned prophet is paradoxically the one who is not abandoned by His Father. In his very weakness he finds his greatest strength (2 Cor. 12:10; Heb. 11:34). He is a pilgrim moving toward the Promised Land and yet at that very moment of abandoning himself to God's loving presence in the present moment he has arrived before his Father's throne. It is in the desert of his poverty and sterility that man allows God to turn the desert into a new spring. The abandoned child, the trusting prophet becomes truly the spouse of Christ called into deeper and deeper union with the Bridegroom.

Come then, my love, my lovely one, come.
Rise up, my love, my fair one and come away.
For lo, the winter is past,
The rain is over and gone.
The flowers appear on the earth.
The time of the singing of birds is come,
And the voice of the turtle is heard in our land. . .
Arise, my love, my fair one and come away. . .
For let me see thy countenance.
Let me hear thy voice.
For sweet is thy voice,
And thy countenance is comely (Song of Songs: 2:10–14).

15

The Prophet Loves

"A new commandment I give unto you that you love one another, even as I have loved you, that you also love one another. By this shall all men know that you are My disciples, if you have love one to another" (Jn. 13:34—35).

In his play "The Cocktail Party" T. S. Eliot has powerfully satirized our capitalistic society that has made human beings into impersonalized ants, very efficiently running their colonies, but knowing no true human communication, knowing little of true love.

Celia, the Christ-image of the play, describes in the first act at a cocktail party modern men and their inability to communicate with each other:

Everyone's alone—or so it seems to me. They make noises and think they are talking to each other. They make faces and think they understand each other. And I'm sure they don't.

At the end of the play, two years later, at a similar cocktail party, it is learned that Celia who had become a Catholic nun and missionary had been killed while tending the sick during a native uprising, apparently crucified, very near an ant-hill. Her Christ-like love for the natives, even to the point of dying for them, produces a tonic effect on those at the party. They seem able, in the light of her heroic love, to open up to each other better than before.

Modern man, in a pragmatic society that is seeking ever more commodities to buy, receive, possess, feels more and more his isolation from his fellow-man. He is desperately lonely and hungers for genuine love. Yet his society has taught him only to receive things. He looks eagerly to "fall in love" with another. Yet he soon finds all too often that he was looking for something to buy, receive, possess and he stalks off looking for new conquests.

Psychologists such as Harry S. Sullivan and Erich Fromm have stressed the process of becoming a person. Man becomes a "realized" human being only through healthy love relationships with others. They point out man's psychological needs for loving relationships. They can analyze conditions of society that prevent man from being a truly loving person. But there is an emptiness when they seek to propose a solution.

The Christian realizes from experience the law of sin in his members. Yet his solution is rooted in Jesus Christ who, by His death on the Cross, has put to death sin in us and raised us up to be children of God. Modern man just as ancient man is incapable by his own fragmented, sinful nature to rise to the heights of a fully realized human being. He is in need of the greatest healing. He tends by nature to be isolated, selective in his love, manipulating others when difficulties arise. But "God is love," says St. John (I Jn. 4:16), and only by His divine life of love living in us can we love as we ought.

JESUS CHRIST AS GOD'S AGAPE

The New Testament uses the Greek word *agape* to describe the revelation of God's love for men, especially in

Christ Jesus. It does not mean that such love never existed before the Word was made flesh and revealed to us the immense love of God for us. God's very nature is to be out-pouring, self-giving toward another. Within the Trinity from all eternity the Father pours His whole being into His Son. The Divine Son receives the fullness of the Father. The Father holds nothing back, for if He did, He would not be the perfect, full source of being. Not His frag-mented needs or dependence on another dictates His self-sacrificing love; only His holiness and goodness that are ordered by love to be shared by Another—His Son.

The Son is constantly receiving and returning this love back to the Father through the personalized, relation-al Love called the Holy Spirit. Paul Tillich expresses in modern terms of self-actualization this Trinitarian mystery rooted in God's movement of love. God the Father, containing an infinity of potentiality, breathes forth His outpouring Spirit of Love and in that Love God's Logos becomes the realized Meaning of God. The Spirit is God's Love through whom God goes out of Himself toward Another, the Logos, and returns to unity through His fulfillment in His Logos, His perfect Image.

But in the Incarnation God's Logos, the actualized Meaning of God, becomes flesh and actualizes in time God's meaning through His Spirit as Love. God's perfect love, *agape*, was brought into human terms. God now could love as total God and yet also He was a total man loving by suffering and dying for each of us. In Jesus Christ we have the perfect love of God actualized. He is the Image of the Father according to whom all human beings have been created (Gen. 1:26).

Thus God's infinite love for man is seen in the loving Jesus of Nazareth. Because He was the perfect Image of the invisible Father (Col. 1:15), as Jesus Christ loves us so the Father loves each of us. "He that has seen Me has seen the Father" (Jn. 14:9). While moving about in Palestine, He was compassionate on the crowds who were like sheep without a shepherd. He cured all the sick and maimed who believed He could heal them. He consoled the afflicted; to all He preached the "Good News" that He had come to bring peace to all. How full of love are His parables of the lost sheep, the Good Samaritan, the Prodigal Son. He had a preference for the poor, the lowly, the sinners. He called Himself "their friend." He loved them with that tender love that a mother has for her children when they are sick. Before He dies for all men on the Cross, He gives them the Holy Eucharist whereby men can feed on His Body and drink His Blood. Finally He acts out in the most poignant manner possible to human communication His infinite love for us by emptying Himself totally on the cross, even to the last drop of water and blood. Almighty God has reached the limit in human language of expressing His illimitable love for man!

A NEW COMMANDMENT OF LOVE

Jesus came among men to send them His Spirit of Love through whom they would be able to call out "Abba! Father!" (Rom. 8:15; Gal. 4:6). The Christian who accepts Jesus Christ as his Savior is a new creation. "If any man be in Christ, he is a new creature; old things are passed away. Behold, all things are become new" (2 Cor. 5:17). This is the exciting Good News that must be preached from the housetops! God so loves us as to make us totally over again. As His Son is by nature, we become sons of God by participation (2 Pet. 1:4). We can rejoice "because the love of God is shed abroad in our hearts by the Holy Spirit who is given unto us" (Rom. 5:5).

Jesus had guaranteed us that "as the Father has loved Me, so have I loved you. Continue in My love" (Jn. 15:9). He promises us that He and the Father will come and abide in us. "If a man love Me, he will keep My words; and My Father will love him and We will come unto him and make Our abode with him" (Jn. 14:23). That very love of God is within the baptized Christian, empowering him to love with God's very own love.

The modern prophet has received from the Holy Spirit a powerful infusion to be able to live within that loving Trinitarian Family. He knows that if he is to love all who enter into his life, it is because of the abiding power of God, loving within him. "If we love one another, God dwells in us and His love is perfected in us. . . And we have known and believed the love that God has for us. God is love; and he that dwells in love dwells in God and God in him" (I Jn. 4:12, 16). The love of Christ has gained control in his life (2 Cor. 5:14—15). He lives no longer for himself, by his own power, but it is now the power of Jesus Christ that lives and operates in his life (Gal. 2:20).

Like St. Paul, the modern-day prophet burns with love for Jesus Christ. He seeks only Him and considers all else as worthless but to possess Him and His love more and more. Yet he wishes to be spent for love of others because it is really the love of Jesus Christ, the Good Shepherd, pursuing again the lost sheep, the sinners who have strayed from the Heavenly Father. Such a love for Christ urges him to spend himself relentlessly to bring others to Christ. Love for another seeks to alleviate all physical sufferings possible from the lives of one's brothers, wherever they may be, whoever they may be. He gives to the hungry and the thirsty, he clothes the naked, he visits and comforts the sick and the imprisoned because he knows the love of Christ within him drives him to love the Christ in his brothers (Matt. 25:35).

Yet he knows from experience the great joy of living in Christ Jesus. He understands what an eternity with Christ for one human being would be and his love increases to bring all men to the knowledge of Jesus as Lord and Savior. With St. Paul, he makes himself a servant unto all in order to gain them for Christ.

> And unto the Jews I became as a Jew that I might gain the Jews; to them that are under the law, as under the law, that I might gain them that are under the law. To them that are without law, as without law (being not without law to God, but under the law to Christ), that I might gain them that are without law. To the weak became I as weak, that I might gain the weak. I am made all things to all men, that I might by all means save some (1 Cor. 9:20–22).

THE QUALITIES OF TRUE LOVE

The prophet, in whom Jesus Christ lives and through whom He loves this world, yields himself more completely each day to the transforming power of Jesus' Spirit, living within him. The two commandments that Jesus Christ is constantly demanding of him are to love God with his whole heart and to love his neighbor as himself. As he looks into the eyes of each person whom he encounters, all walls of separation tumble as by his look he says: "I am your brother. I love you! You are beautiful in God's love. How can I serve you?"

He knows from experience that true love is a dying to his own narcissism or self-love that is turned in upon himself. Yet it is a finding of his true self in serving the other. In giving he receives, yet he seeks only to give. He puts no price tag on his loving service.

St. Paul characterizes in one of the most beautiful literary passages in Holy Scripture what true love is. One could possess great gifts of prophecy, of understanding all mysteries, of knowing all knowledge, of faith so strong it could move mountains; one could give millions of dollars to the poor, even give up his own body to be burned, but if he has not *love*, his other talents and good works are of no value.

> Love suffers long and is kind. Love envies not. Love vaunts not itself, is not puffed up. It does not behave itself unseemly, seeks not its own, is not easily provoked, thinks no evil. It rejoices not in iniquity, but rejoices in the truth. Love bears all things, believes all things, hopes all things, endures all things. Love never fails (1 Cor. 13:4–8).

The prophet seeks to live this kind of love in every encounter with each person. He praises God for the successes in others; he sees the goodness in each person. He is disciplined to control his "gut" reactions toward others, putting all ill feelings of hurt pride, envy, jealousy, anger under the healing power of Jesus Christ living within him. He is basically *humble* in his proper love of self which means in its essence a love that is "toward others." He never hurts anyone; "love never fails" to forgive, overlook, pass over in silence, to seek to serve the needs of others. Love allows the modern prophet to see only God in himself and in others and he experiences also that God sees Himself truly in him, not only as the operating force of true love, making it possible for him to love all with complete openness to serve but also as mirrored forth in the Image of Jesus Christ who has become one with him.

Is this not the end of all of our lives? To become prophets of love who experience in the core of our beings Jesus Christ living and transforming us into children of God? Are we not called by God's grace into that intimate union with Jesus Christ that there is only He loving in us? Our progress in prayer and ultimately our full maturity in God is measured by the consciousness we have that Jesus Christ is totally one with us. We surrender at each moment our whole being to be operated by His loving power. Our will over our life, thoughts, words, actions is now surrendered totally to His.

St. Symeon the New Theologian beautifully expresses this conscious union with Christ in all of man's members:

> We become members of Christ and Christ becomes
>   our members,
> Christ becomes my hand, Christ, my miserable foot;
>   and I, unhappy one, am Christ's hand, Christ's foot!
> I move my hand and my hand is the whole Christ
>   since, do not forget it, God is indivisible in His divinity.
> I move my foot and behold it shines like That One!
> Do not accuse me of blasphemy, but welcome these
>   things and adore Christ who makes you such since,
>   if you so wish, you will become a member of Christ
>   and similarly all our members individually will become
>   members of Christ and Christ our members, and all
>   which is dishonorable in us He will make honorable
>   by adorning it with His divine beauty and His divine
>   glory, since living with God at the same time, we shall
>   become gods, no longer seeing the shamefulness of
>   our body at all, but made completely like Christ in our
>   whole body, each member of our body will be the
>   whole Christ.
> . . .It is truly a marriage which takes place, ineffable
>   and divine;
> God unites Himself with each one—yes, I repeat it,

It is my delight—and each one becomes one with the
Master (Hymn 15).

The prophet not only is aware that Jesus Christ lives
in him, directing him to praise and glorify the Heavenly
Father, but he also points out to the world the inner loving
presence of God in each human encounter. God is always
revealing Himself as love, communicating Himself in each
human relationship. No one can anticipate God's self-
giving by describing the circumstances or the degree of His
love in each meeting.

The prophet is attentive and open, ready to cor-
respond with love for God's love. His faith in God's loving
presence finds Him everywhere. His trust allows him to
surrender himself totally to the concrete situation. The
infused love of the Holy Spirit allows him to give himself
in delicate sensitivity to the "other."

Teilhard de Chardin addresses himself to Jesus Christ
as such a modern prophet eager to love Him in the human
encounter:

. . .my heart cannot reach Your person except at the depths of
all that is most individually and concretely personal in every
'other'—it is to the 'other' himself, and not to some vague
entity around him, that my charity is addressed. . .You
merely, through Your revelation and Your grace, force what is
most human in me to become conscious of itself at last.
Humanity was sleeping—it is still sleeping—imprisoned in
the narrow joys of its little closed loves. A tremendous
spiritual power is slumbering in the depths of our multitude which will manifest itself only when we have learnt
to break down the barriers of our egoisms and, by a
fundamental recasting of our outlook, raise ourselves up
to the habitual and practical vision of universal realities
(Divine Milieu).

The modern prophet goes through his world not so much telling others of God's great love but pointing out the loving energy of God in every circumstance. He releases this loving energy like a great hydro-electric dam that opens its valves to let in the pent up waters to turn turbines that will produce power.

This loving power is God's very own life, transforming the world into light and heat, the light that allows each human being to "see" God loving us human beings in each situation and the heat to warm our human hearts to adore the almighty, tender loving God as we lovingly open ourselves to serve one another.

> Beloved, let us love one another; for love is of God, and everyone that loves is born of God and knows God (1 Jn. 4:7).

16

The Prophet Suffers and Dies

"Whosoever will lose his life for My sake shall find it" (Matt. 16:25).

There are many things that we can be *anti-*. We can be anti-war, anti-pollution, anti-poverty. But one thing a prophet cannot be is *anti-spring*! This would be equivalent to being anti-hope and anti-new life. Spring is the most basic perennial experience in man's life of the beginning of new life. After a long, dull winter during which frost and snow have stripped nature of all signs of verdant life and covered each created thing with the sign of cold death, spring comes with its clarion call of hope that announces that what lay so many months in apparent death is about to stir unto new, fresh life.

There is a fundamental law in nature that could be formulated in these words: "There is nothing that lives that something must die. There is nothing that dies but that something else will live." Jesus Christ taught this law many times in quite blunt language. He had seen in his growing years in Nazareth the sower that sowed seed in spring. And so He taught:

Unless the grain of wheat falls into the ground and dies, it abides alone. But if it dies, it brings forth much fruit. He that loves his life shall lose it. And he that hates his life in this world shall keep it unto life enternal (Jn. 12:24—25).

When the seed seems most at the point of death, that germ of life bursts through the dead shell pushing up through the earth a green sprout of fresh life. In paradoxical language Jesus insisted that if any one wanted to be His disciple and obtain eternal life, he had to begin by a "dying" process. He had to enter into a suffering, but one that would deliver him unto new life. He had to take the risk of surrendering himself to Him by giving up a lower level of existence which allowed him to be in dominance, ruling his own life, to accept Christ's offer to move unto a higher level of existence to be guided by His Holy Spirit. Thus Jesus taught the necessity of his prophet to deny himself, to suffer and in a way to die. But this suffering and dying were the stepping stones to a new life.

> If any man will come after Me, let him deny himself and take up his cross and follow Me. For whosoever will save his life shall lose it. And whoever will lose his life for My sake shall find it (Matt. 16:24–25; Mk. 8:34–35; Lk. 9:23–24).

It is interesting to note that the fact that this same passage is nearly verbatim found in all three Synoptic accounts would indicate that the early Christian teaching, received from Jesus, held this doctrine on self-denial unto new life as an essential part of the Christian message.

But more importantly Jesus lived this law out in His own earthly life. The Gospel accounts of His earthly life present it in terms of the *Exodus*. He was passing over from death unto life everlasting. The Greek Fathers were fond of calling the Savior of the world, the *sperma logikon*, the Logos Seed of Divine Life that was inserted into our suffering and sinful humanity. The soldiers on Calvary lifted that Divine Seed aloft and then plunged it into the hole prepared for it in the earth. Its whole side was split and at the very moment that the Seed seemed to have perished, an inner life burst forth into a new and glorious eternal life. Jesus was risen on Calvary! He was glorified by the Father in that moment that He cried out triumphantly and joyful: "It is consummated. Father into Thy hands I commend My spirit!"

A CHRISTIAN MEANING TO SUFFERING

Suffering will be the lot of every human being. Whether he accepts it or not, he will still have to bear a great deal of suffering. As Job found out, suffering will always remain a mystery to man's puny reasoning powers. But Jesus Christ came to give to His disciples a vision of faith and the strength through His indwelling life to "suffer with Him that we may be also glorified together" (Rom. 8:17).

Man suffers passively in the mere act of growing from infancy to childhood, from being a youth to reaching the full maturity of adulthood. There are biological, psychological and spiritual sufferings that "happen" to us and are necessary if we are to grow more fully on the levels of body, soul and spirit relationships. There will be the sufferings of sickness, the bunglings of ourselves and those of others acting upon us, the doubts, fears and anxieties from our own creatureliness and sinfulness to cope with the many problems of life. Ultimately there will be the greatest diminishment of death itself to lead us into the final, physical suffering in order to pass into eternal life.

There will be sufferings on a more active level of working in the sweat of our brow for our daily bread. This will entail much discipline and above all much monotony. It calls for a usual, banal routine that in the ultimate analysis cuts away at our egoism as we learn to transcend the momentarily monotonous into a larger vision of creative labor.

Perhaps the greatest call to suffering comes from what apparently should be the most pleasant: from human love. Man grows most as a human being when he is called out by another human person to forget and surrender himself for that person in true, self-sacrificing love. Love is an invitation to suffer, for it means to say "yes" to another and entailed in this acceptance to love is a "no" to any conflicting selfishness.

Here we can easily see from our personal experience that the more one advances in true love and union with another, the more he is also called to relinquish his own self-centered world and to believe and trust and love the other. The marriage in which the husband or wife do the minimum will soon be no marriage at all. True love moves beyond justice and the demands of the law into an inner direction that is based on reverence for the other. The husband seeks to please the wife and the wife the husband by seeking to do always the wish of the other. But at the heart of a successful love-relationship such as should be found in marriage man and woman must partake of a generosity that is built upon creative suffering which we call *sacrifice.*

TO LOVE IS TO SACRIFICE ONESELF

The prophet in today's world that is so materialistic and exploiting of others gradually learns in his experience of God's Word that true love is built on sacrifice. In his love for Christ he can say with St. Paul:

> I count all things but loss for the excellency of the knowledge
> of Christ Jesus my Lord, for whom I have suffered the loss of
> all things and do count them but dung that I may win
> Christ...that I may know Him and the power of His
> resurrection and the fellowship of His sufferings, being made
> comformable unto His death, if by any means I might attain
> unto the resurrection of the dead (Phil. 3:8—11).

He knows that Jesus Christ through His sufferings has
made him a part of a holy people. "God should make the
Leader of their salvation a perfect leader through the fact
that He suffered" (Heb. 2:10). Jesus has suffered, "leaving
us an example that you should follow His steps" (1 Pet.
2:21).

The word *sacrifice* comes from the Latin: *sacrum
facere*; to make something sacred, to consecrate or to set
aside for a holy purpose. The modern world fears anything
that calls for self-sacrifice. It looks upon men and women
who "sacrifice," set aside as holy offering to God, for
example, their sexual powers, the most beautiful gift that
God has given them through which they can grow in true,
human self-surrender to another, as non-profitable human
beings. Such a consecration is only negative, a loss, an
unprofit to the world in their eyes. They fail to see instead
the creative suffering out of love in order to give oneself to
God and to others in a more immediate self-surrender in
loving service.

The modern prophet in contemplating his suffering
Savior on the cross begins to understand through the
power of the Holy Spirit what cannot be understood by a
man of the world. He enters into the "folly of the Cross"
that is such a stumbling block for the Jews and the
Gentiles. He has "the mind of Christ" (1 Cor. 2:16) to
understand that the "foolishness of God is wiser than men

and the weakness of God is stronger than men. . .But God has chosen the foolish things of the world to confound the wise and God has chosen the weak things of the world to confound the things which are mighty" (1 Cor. 1:25–27).

The horrendous folly of the Cross of Christ is sheer wasted pain except in terms of the logic of love! The prophet realizes that Jesus could have redeemed the world by dying and the awful *kenosis* or self-emptying, even to the last drop of blood and water, lies in the gift of a free love offering, a self-sacrifice for each human being. "Ought not Christ to have suffered these things and to enter into His glory?" (Lk. 24:26). Man would have always entertained some doubt as to the infinite love of God who so loved us as to give us His only begotten Son (Jn. 3:16) unless Jesus had gone all the way! In the Cross of Jesus Christ the prophet sees the ultimate in God's self-surrendering sacrifice for man. God Himself in all His omnipotence reaches a limit, an end to His ability to convey to finite man His infinite love in human language, the language of creative suffering even unto death.

The prophet in meditating on the suffering Jesus is moved to a like generosity. Love experienced calls out a similar love. He knows that he cannot be under the law alone in his response to God's great love for himself in Christ Jesus. Under the Spirit he moves to a delicacy of conscience that seeks always, as Jesus Himself did, to do the will of the Heavenly Father. "Not my will but Thine be done!" (Lk. 22:42). He goes even farther and here the prophet in imitating the sufferings of Christ takes his place among those weak ones that God has called to be His instruments of power in this world, His saints, made holy by the power of the sanctifying Holy Spirit. He seeks to "improvise" ways of suffering with Christ that His Body may be filled with glory. His co-suffering with Christ makes the words of St. Paul a reality and still a mystery of divine love at work in his soul:

> Who now rejoice in my sufferings for you and fill up that which is behind of the afflictions of Christ in my flesh for his body's sake which is the Church (Col. 1:24).

TOWARD OTHERS

The love of God turns the prophet toward the suffering world. The compassion of Jesus for the multitudes becomes his suffering as he pleads to God in intercessory prayer. He burns firstly out of love for God and mankind to become a part of a "holy priesthood to offer up spiritual sacrifices acceptable to God by Jesus Christ" (1 Pet. 2:5). In the Old and also in the New Testaments we find that the anointing into the priesthood of the Lord is one of setting oneself aside for spiritual sacrifices. The priest was to be holy as God is holy. This meant that he was to separate himself from all uncleanliness. There was to be a purification and an emptying so that he would be totally at the service of God. He was to be "without spot or blemish" (Ephes. 5:27), "the man of God perfect, thoroughly furnished unto all good works" (2 Tim. 2:7).

The prophet learns to suffer creatively in order to be holy unto the Lord, but he suffers also in his intercession for mankind. He suffers in the works of ministering to others, in the trials, persecutions, lack of cooperation that he receives from them. He suffers in his burning love for all men that they may be brought to the full knowledge of Christ Jesus. He shortens his sleep to stand in adoration and in intercession for the needs of his fellow-men. He is ready to pay any price, as St. Paul confessed, that others may know Jesus Christ. He dies to his own comfort and wants to live that Jesus be Lord in the lives of all men. No sacrifice in prayer, fasting or personal dying to self is too great to gain all men to Christ.

ABIDE IN ME

It is a continued experience in the life of the modern prophet that without Jesus and the power of the Holy Spirit working in his life he is nothing. Jesus is the vine; he is the branch.

> Abide in Me and I in you. As the branch cannot bear fruit of itself, except it abide in the vine, no more can you, except you abide in Me (Jn. 15:4).

The Heavenly Father is the Vinedresser and He prunes those whom He loves. The pruning is not an end in itself but it is that the branch may bring forth more fruit (Jn. 15:2). There can be no abiding in Jesus except through a pruning of selfishness. But if there is this abiding then the prophet attached to Christ will bear much fruit.

It is interesting to note that in another context of much fruit-bearing, Jesus had earlier spoken of the necessity of the seed of grain falling into the ground and dying. Death to self on the one hand and abiding with Jesus Christ on the other result in both cases with much fruit being brought forth. Such Christian suffering is not morbid, masochistic or unreal. It is at the heart of the reality we call love, love of God and love of neighbor.

This dying process is not what produces God's fruit. Only the Spirit can bring forth the fruit of the Father: His shared life with the sons of God. It is the necessary emptying as dispositive in order that the full power of the Spirit can work in the prophet. Then the prophet, abiding in such intimate union with Jesus Lord, will find His words to be true:

> You have not chosen Me, but I have chosen you and ordained you that you should go and bring forth fruit and that your fruit should remain; that whatsoever you shall ask of the Father in My name, He may give it you (Jn. 15:16).

O DEATH, WHERE IS THY STING?

Suffering is a spiritual and a psychological death of a sort to our own egoism in order that Jesus Christ can be full Master and Lord. But the prophet today performs his greatest role before the world as an eschatological witness that there is life eternal beyond the physical death for those who love the Lord. His faith in Jesus Christ who has conquered over sin and death is so great that even as he lives, but above all in the moment of his own death he knows with assurance that in the words of the Prophet Isaiah:

> He will swallow up death in victory. And the Lord God will wipe away tears from off all faces (Is. 25:8).

The modern prophet witnesses to a pragmatic world, that measures reality in terms of present quantitative power or pleasure, that God, through Jesus Christ, has entered into death and has conquered it in Christ's humanity. The prophet has put on Christ. He lives in and with Christ. Hence Christ's power is in him also overcoming corruption and sin. With the Prophet Hosea he can shout out the words of the Promised Messiah: "I will ransom them from the power of the grave. I will redeem them from death. O death, I will be thy plagues. O grave, I will be thy destruction" (Hos. 13:14). St. Paul was thinking in these words when he wrote:

> So when this corruptible shall have put on incorruption and this mortal shall have put on immortality, then shall be brought to pass the saying that is written: Death is swallowed up in victory. O death, where is they sting? O grave, where is thy victory? The sting of death is sin and the strength of sin is the law. But thanks be to God who gives us the victory through our Lord Jesus Christ (1 Cor. 15:54–57).

The prophet of Jesus Christ lives a constant death to self. "I die each day" (1 Cor. 15:31). He reaches a spiritual maturity of being so united to God that nothing in life or death can ever separate him from the love of Christ Jesus (Rom. 8:38). He enjoys a security and certitude, not in any reliance on his good works, not in any magical way of having once and for all been saved, but in the conscious experience that the Heavenly Father has placed His power and blessings in him (Jn. 13:3). He begins even now in this pilgrimage on earth, while still in the corruptible body, to experience something of immortality, incorruptibility, the unchangeability of God's eternal love for him.

The Holy Spirit constantly sheds His divine light upon him to enlighten him to see all things in God's original plan. He is unmoved by opinions or fancies of men. All events are seen in the light of eternity. For such a Christian the Risen Jesus is a continued experience even now. He can mock death that received its hold on mankind through sin.

Knowing that Christ being raised from the dead dies no more, death has no more dominion over him. For in that He died, He died unto sin once. But in that He lives, He lives unto God. Likewise reckon you also yourselves to be dead indeed unto sin, but alive unto God through Jesus Christ our Lord (Rom. 6:9-11).

This is the integrated human being, the man made free of all fear, especially the greatest, the fear of final death. Such a prophet witnesses in every word and gesture that Jesus Christ is risen and dies no more. And if He be risen, so he also even now shares in that risen life. He shares his vision of hope and joy with all who are heavily burdened with suffering, above all, with those in sin and in the throes of final death. He shows that he has passed from death unto life "because we love the brethren" (1 Jn. 3:14). He strives at each moment to live in the commandments of Jesus Christ. "If any man keeps My saying, he shall never see death" (Jn.8:51). Obedience to Jesus Christ is the answer he gives to the world to suffering and dying.

17

The Prophet "Sees" God By Faith

"The life which I now live in the flesh I live by the faith of the Son of God, who loved me and gave Himself for me" (Gal. 2:20).

Man is born into this world unable to see God and yet God is everywhere. Like a man physically blind who gropes and feels his way toward the real world around him, listens to clues of joys and sufferings to be embraced or avoided, so all of us seek to contact God who is all around us, yet we cannot see Him. A Christian becomes a prophet through God's gift of faith. He becomes a gifted human being, a "seer" capable of seeing God present to this world and hearing His communication to His People.

He can show the rest of blinded humanity what they fail to see. He can lead them also out of their blindness by his sure knowledge of faith of the Way that leads to the Truth. How the world needs such prophets who see God by faith! Such prophets see Him in Holy Scripture, in the history of salvation and reveal to the present world that the same living God of Abraham, Isaac and Jacob is faithful to His Chosen People. They see love of God incarnated in Jesus Christ who now is gloriously risen and inserted by His living presence in every atom of the material world. They see this Jesus of Nazareth still multiplying the loaves, the Bread of Life, and giving

Himself as food and drink in the Holy Eucharist. They see Him within the Church, the people who are bound by the Holy Spirit's love in a community of service to extend Jesus Christ as the Light of the world. They see Him in the teaching authority within the Church.

They have learned to see Him in each person they meet, in each human activity and event of each day. Jesus Christ is shining diaphanously throughout the whole world for those who have the eyes to see, writes Teilhard de Chardin in his *Divine Milieu*. They shout out their discoveries to men whose spiritual eyes are covered with heavy shades of darkness. They above all share their gift of faith by instructing others how to have their spiritual eyes opened to see God as they do.

THE GIFT OF FAITH

Once when Jesus entered the town of Bethsaida a blind man was brought to him to be healed. St. Mark's Gospel records some strange details in this miraculous healing.

> And he took the blind man by the hand and led him out of the town; and when He had spit on his eyes and put His hands upon him, He asked him if he saw. And he look up and said, 'I see men as trees, walking.' After that He put His hands again upon his eyes and made him look up. And he was restored and saw every man clearly (Mk. 8:23–25).

In one of his homilies St. John Chrysostom makes a comparison between the rock out of which came the living water that brought life to God's Chosen People in the desert and Jesus Christ whose saliva from His mouth brought sight to the blind man. He notes that Jesus drew the blind man out of the town, signifying the necessity of a conversion of heart, a turning away from the familiar and fixed ways of looking on life. Jesus then gradually restores his sight. He first sees men as trees or objects. Then we are told he sees every man clearly. The faith moves from a vision of darkness to shadows to see finally human beings and all of creation clearly as they exist in God's plan.

St. Thomas Aquinas said that the end of man is to contemplate God. Faith is that gift of the Holy Spirit infused into God's children who seek it and want it that allows man even now to see God everywhere.

The modern prophet sees his life and the lives of all men as imperfect and unfulfilled, lacking in true maturity without this gift of faith. Human maturity is based on man's sincerity and honesty to strive to live according to truth as far as he sees it. An immature person refuses to accept the reality that he is such a kind of person with some good qualities as well as some failings. An honest man genuinely accepts himself and others as they are. Such a person is capable of moving toward greater maturity through the love that he is able to offer another. Through that giving and receiving, he enters into a sense of self-identity.

Faith in an excellent way offers the modern prophet the maturity that comes from a knowledge from God of the supremacy of God in his life and of his own finiteness and utter dependence upon Him. Through faith he is open to God's love, especially as revealed in Jesus Christ and His loving presence in other human beings. The Holy Spirit through faith convicts the prophet of faith of his true self-identity. He is loved by God, made by the Holy Spirit a true child of God and belongs to a community of brothers and sisters who are co-heirs of Heaven forever with Jesus Christ.

The prophet who sees God in places where most people see nothing is led through his faith into a freedom that all men seek. Jesus had said: "If you remain in My word, you are truly My disciples. And you will know the truth and the truth will make you free" (Jn. 8:31–32). Faith in the freeing power of the Word of God brings the disciples of Jesus Christ a freedom from fear for they never walk this earth alone. They "see" that Jesus Christ is within them, guiding them by His Holy Spirit to a right knowledge of the Way. They are freed from themselves, from the false images and masks people usually put on to "win friends and influence people." They are freed from the erroneous popular opinions about God, the world, ultimate values and themselves that other people entertain. Faith gives a freedom from the darkness of past sins and scared memories that haunt and cripple most people and force them to live joyless lives, enslaved to the past.

Such freedom through the gift of faith is already a share in happiness that grows in a sense of security in possessing and seeing God, even now, and of belonging to His family. This buoys up the Christian with an unflagging hope that overcomes all obstacles.

GROWTH IN SEEING GOD

Faith that allows us to see God in each event at each moment comes to us first through preaching and instruction that are rooted in the Word of God. It is the Church's obligation to teach and instruct the faithful that their faith in Jesus Christ and their Heavenly Father who send them Their Holy Spirit of love may continuously grow stronger.

St. Paul's insistence on this point is still applicable to all of us today:

> How then shall they call on Him in whom they have not believed? And how shall they believe in Him of whom they have not heard? And how shall they hear without a preacher? And how shall they preach except they be sent? As it is written, 'How beautiful are the feet of them that preach the gospel of peace and bring glad tidings of good things!'. . .So then faith comes by hearing and hearing by the word of God (Rom. 10:14–17).

Jesus Christ is still speaking to us through the written words of Holy Scripture. Thus our faith in His Good News and His healing power becomes strengthened also through a prayerful study of Holy Scripture. In such contact with Jesus Christ we are able today at any time to "put on the mind of Christ." He speaks through Holy Scripture but as a Person still living and communicating with us, from within our very being.

Our faith is built up also by the witness of other Christians to the presence of Jesus Christ in their lives. It is an applied, personalized form of preaching, instructing, and studying the Holy Scripture by hearing from other Christians of vibrant faith. The modern prophet believes God speaks through the testimony of sincere Christians who share their faith-vision with him. He also shares what the Lord does in his personal life, all that the Body of Christ might be built up and grow stronger.

Faith in the presence and loving work of Jesus Christ grows especially in the encounter of the Christian with Christ directly in the sacraments. For most adults these are mainly the healing and reconciling sacrament of Penance and the peak of mutual self-surrender of God and man in the Holy Eucharist. Actually the modern prophet begins to "see" that the sacramental activity of Jesus Christ cannot be confined merely to the few minutes during which the sacrament is being received. Baptism, for example, becomes for him a continued process of going down into the darkness and chaos of his inner self, typified by water, to rise through a spiritual cleansing to a new life in Christ Risen. The Christian is always being "introduced" into the community of faith-believers, the Church, and thereby living His Baptism he encounters more deeply the living Christ in the midst of his fellow believers. To live one's Baptism is to live according to the dignity that was given the Christian in the first moment of his Baptism that continues to grow as he lives a life of transformation into a true child of God. Baptism leads the Christian always to Penance and the need to ask and receive forgiveness and healing from the Divine Physician.

FAITH IN THE EUCHARIST

But the modern prophet's faith finds its peak of development in the Holy Eucharist. Here is where he comes into full contact with the risen and glorified Jesus Christ. If Jesus Christ speaks to him through the preaching and teaching and witnessing of others of deep knowledge and faith, in the Eucharist He is most fully and most directly speaking and giving Himself to the Christian. Faith reaches the fullness of "seeing" Jesus Christ in the Divine Liturgy that builds up in a microcosmic way all the prior ways discussed above. The Christian joins other Christians and their faith is shared together. They cry out for forgiveness and healing. The Word of God is preached and explained. Through faith they pray together, begging God to answer their needs in the prayers of the faithful, thanking and praising God for all His gifts in the Preface and Canon. But in the Consecration and Communion their faith reaches the climax of "seeing" Jesus Christ directly and immediately. Teilhard prays a Eucharistic prayer in the *Divine Milieu*:

> Grant, O God that when I draw near to the altar to communicate, I may henceforth discern the infinite perspectives hidden beneath the smallness and the nearness of the Host in which You are concealed. I have already accustomed myself to seeing, beneath the stillness of that piece of bread, a devouring power which, in the words of the greatest Doctors of Your Church, far from being consumed by me, consumes me. Give me the strength to rise above the remaining illusions which tend to make me think of Your touch as circumscribed and momentary.

> I am beginning to understand: under the sacramental Species it is primarily through the 'accidents' of matter that You touch me, but, as a consequence, it is also through the whole universe in proportion as this ebbs and flows over me under Your primary influence. In a true sense the arms and the heart which You open to me are nothing less than all the united powers of the world which, penetrated and permeated to their depths by Your will, Your tastes and Your temperament, converge upon my being to form it, nourish it and bear it along towards the center of Your fire. In the Host it is my life that You are offering me, O Jesus.

The Eucharist is not merely a moment in time in which we meet Jesus Christ and "see" Him transforming us into His Body, although this action takes place in a series of moments through our lives. Through the vision of faith experienced when the Christian fervently receives Jesus in Holy Communion, the prophet "sees" Jesus Christ also hidden under the species of the whole material world. The Eucharistic prophet leaves the Divine Liturgy with an increase of faith that allows him to see Jesus Christ, not only in the bread and wine transfigured in the Liturgy, but he sees His sacred presence hidden in the whole material world of other species of bread and wine: sufferings and joys, mountains and valleys, rivers and oceans. He sees that the whole world "lives and moves and has its being" (Acts 17:28) in Him. Teilhard again has well captured the cosmic dimension of the Eucharistic Lord when he writes: ". . . the Eucharistic transformation goes beyond and completes the transubstantiation of the bread on the altar. Step by step it irresistibly invades the universe. It is the fire that sweeps over the heath; the stroke that vibrates through the bronze. In a secondary and generalized sense, but in a true sense, the sacramental Species are formed by the totality of the world and the duration of the creation is the time needed for its consecration" *(Divine Millieu)*.

The modern prophet with enlivened faith in the pervading presence of Jesus Christ in the entire universe adores Him in the context of experiencing Him in his daily life. He seeks as he does in the moments of Eucharistic adoration to surrender himself to the divinizing transfiguring process of Jesus Christ upon himself and, through him in his priestly action of working on matter, upon the whole material world.

REFLECTIVE SEEING

Growth in discovering the dynamic, creating energies of God in every facet of life is a life process. But the true prophet knows that he must find moments to reflect on this presence of God within the concrete context of his daily life. Without reflection on the daily contact with God in the existential word that God has been speaking in a given day, the Christian soon finds his faith in God's presence relegated only to the Eucharist or to Holy Scripture. The total Jesus Christ in all His loving presence in each moment is not seen. One's faith weakens.

To grow, therefore, in this "seeing" of God in all events, the prophet learns to sit quietly before the Lord, especially at the end of each day and gaze at Him, see Him, look at Him as He has involved Himself in His Trinitarian relationships of love in man's activities of that day. Such a "seer" praises God, giving thanks for His great love and His many gifts of that day. He becomes sensitive and soon thanks God for gifts that before were seen as obstacles and mere negative crosses. He begs illumination from the Holy Spirit of love to pierce through the darkness of a lack of faith to see God and to see himself in relation to the loving Lord.

He reviews the day under God's eyes, seeing behind the bread and wine of each moment the Eucharistic Lord, giving Himself as food and drink. He praises God when he "saw" God and adored Him by cooperating with His holy will. He sees with honest regret and remorse where his selfishness blinded him to God's gift of Himself in the concrete circumstances of the past day. And so he cries out for the healing mercy and loving compassion of the Trinity. He does not exaggerate his sinfulness. He knows from the evident facts, from his living history of that day that he is caught in a contagion of sinfulness and sickness and desperately needs healing. "Lord, Jesus Christ, Son of God, have mercy on me, a sinner!"

As he feels the healing power of Jesus Christ come over him to transform the joys and sufferings of that day into His Body, the modern prophet surrenders himself to the loving energies of God in the day to come. He already begins to pray his offertory of the next day's Divine Liturgy, the cosmic Mass, as he offers to the transfiguring power of the Holy Spirit not only his thoughts, words and actions of tomorrow but he gathers into that offering the whole, needy world. As many grains of wheat went into making bread and many grapes were crushed to make the wine of the Eucharist, so the modern prophet and priest offers the whole world in all of its crying, individual needs and in all of its communal lack of unity.

This is the modern prophet who "sees" God by faith and adores Him by a return of complete surrender to Him who has given the world not only all of its existence and thrust towards greater fullness but above all has given us the Person of Jesus Christ in a vision of faith to see even now that His Body is being formed in us through the life He brings us in the Holy Eucharist. Through our living submission to Him, His life is extended even to the sub-human cosmos, His sacred humanity touches this or that area of the material world to transfigure it into a united Eucharistic hymn of praise to the Eternal Father. The prophet is the priest who "sees" not only trees and men but also Jesus Christ in all things and all things in Him.

18

The Prophet Witnesses to Christ's Transfiguration

"Therefore, if any man be in Christ, he is a new creature. Old things are passed away. Behold, all things are become new" (2 Cor. 5:17).

There is gathering around us, like a huge blanketing cloud of black, suffocating smog, a fear that does not seem to lift and show us the sun. Evils in our societies with increasing violent crimes added to terrifying economic pressures, labor strikes, increasing prices, millions already starving and others fearing the imminent lack of food and essentials for living a properly human life, these are just a few of the elements that are at the basis of this mounting fear.

More than ever before, the world looks to prophets who can lead us to the mountain top and show Jesus Christ transfigured in all His glory with Moses and Elijah at His side. These cannot be mere dreamers or escape artists who, in the trenchant words of Diedrich Bonhoeffer, kick their heels in the face of impending difficulties in life and fly off to that upper region in the heavens where all is peaceful harmony, the home of cowards who make a mockery of true Christianity by their false attitude towards this present world.

One of the principal Christian feasts celebrated in the Byzantine Churches is that of the feast of the Transfiguration on August 6th. The faithful bring to the church their first fruits to be blessed and offered to God in thanksgiving and petition for the bountiful harvest they will soon expect. As they watch the priest bless these first fruits they enter into an act of faith in which they have already participated. They had planted in spring the seeds and pruned the vines and fruit branches in faith that, although they could see absolutely no signs of fruit in the seeds or dead-looking branches, fruit would surely come. Over the hot months they labored in their fields buoyed up by the promise of the harvest to come. The labor would not be equal to the harvest!

But they were witnessing on a deeper religious level to a vision of faith that dealt with an eternal harvest and that of the whole universe. They believed that in their Baptism the life of God had been sown into their very beings as an embryonic life in Christ Jesus. The Trinity lived within them. They were to grow to maturity. A transfiguration process was to take place over the long spring, summer and autumn years of their human lives.

Tied to their own belief that they would one day see their own transfiguration as sons of God and co-heirs with Jesus Christ, they profess that Jesus Christ not only was transfigured on the mountain-top along with Moses and Elijah in the presence of Peter, James and John but that He is now risen and transfigured in glory at the right hand of His Father. God has raised Him to glory and a new life (Acts 2:24). And one day He will also transfigure all of us into sharers of His glorious, risen body. Jesus "shall change our vile body, that it may be fashioned like unto His glorious body according to the working, whereby He is able even to subdue all things unto Himself" (Phil. 3:21).

The greatest fear that cripples most human beings is

that of death. Carlos Castaneda in his book, *Journey to Ixthlan*, has Don Juan, the Mexican shaman in the New Mexican desert, comment on this fear. Man is always putting off living intensely, he says, afraid to make full decisions with the wholeness of his being, because he always thinks he will have more time. A hunter is different. He is besieged by enemies all around. He must be ready to die, but he must more importantly be ready to live, as wanting to live forever. He, therefore, lives each moment as though it were his last, because he believes it will be a *forever* moment.

St. Irenaeus in the 3rd century put it succinctly: "The glory of God is man living fully." Such should be the modern prophet who witnesses not only to the glorious resurrection of Jesus Christ already gloriously reigning forever at the right hand of His Father but also to his own personal resurrection and transfiguration in Christ Jesus, a process that is now going on. He witnesses to the truth that the moment of death is not so important. *This* present moment is all-important. It leads him to the next. Like the seed unfolding its tremendous potential to become the full fruit, he knows that the uncreated energies of the Father and Son and Holy Spirit abide within him, seeking to sweep him into that same glorious life, now and for eternity.

With the Prophet Isaiah he believes that God is even now doing a new thing.

> Behold, I will do a new thing. Now it shall spring forth. Shall you not know it? I will even make a way in the wilderness and rivers in the desert. . .I give waters in the wilderness and rivers in the desert to give drink to My people, My chosen. This people have I formed for Myself. They shall show forth My praise (Is. 43:19—20).

The prophet witnesses to the world today that Jesus is the Resurrection and the Life. "He that believes in Me, though he were dead, yet shall he live. And whosoever lives and believes in Me shall never die" (Jn. 11:25−26).

THE COSMIC CHRIST

But above all, the modern prophet calls all men to believe through Christian hope in the transfiguration process now going on throughout the whole cosmos. Not only human beings but the whole sub-human cosmos is under "the bondage of corruption" (Rom. 8:21) and "we know that the whole creation groans and travails in pain *together* until now" (Rom. 8:22).

God truly loves the world He created. "And God saw that it was good!" (Gen. 1:18). He has created all things, every atom of matter, in and through His Word, Jesus Christ. The modern prophet witnesses to the sustaining presence of God's Logos within all of creation. He is inside of all that exists. "For in Him we live and move and have our being" (Acts 17:28). These energies of God bathe the whole universe and charge it with His infinite love. The Body of Christ is being formed through the priestly ministry of each human being made according to that Image and Likeness that is Jesus Christ and it is being shaped and fashioned by all things material. Although all around us seems in chaotic confusion and life has "no exit" as was Sartre's verdict, the Christian prophet points to the inner, loving presence of the Cosmic Christ within matter, within this crazy world, and shows that there is a divine purpose. Christ is evolving this universe into His Body. He is moving it towards Omega which He is. "I am Alpha and Omega, the beginning and the ending, says the

Lord, which is and which was and which is to come, the Almighty" (Rev. 1:8).

The prophet stands before his people and calls them to their awesome dignity of cooperating with the uncreated energies of God Himself. Creation is not finished. It is on-going. And God calls man to be a "reconciler" of the whole creation through Jesus Christ back to Him. A *synergy* (working with) of creativity between God and man summons out the best in man as he, in total submission to the mind of God, seeks to use his gifts and talents to transfigure this universe into the Heavenly Jerusalem. The prophet sees the pruning hand of God, the pedagogic Divine Master, instructing His children, correcting, admonishing, exhorting in what seems to be, at times, sheer negative evil, physical or moral, for the unbelieving.

Rather than running away from involvement in the activities of this world, the prophet leads his people into the fray. Resurrectional hope is social and historical. What man adds to make this world a better world in Christ Jesus has an eternal effect on the whole process. Man is not resurrected from the body but his resurrection takes place in his spiritualized body. It is not a fresh start but the old is made totally new.

> Therefore if any man be in Christ, he is a new creature. Old things are passed away. Behold, all things are become new. And all things are of God, who has reconciled us to Himself by Jesus Christ and has given to us the ministry of reconciliation (2 Cor. 5:17–18).

The building up of the Body of Christ, the Church, is not the gathering of an elect group out of the human race with the rest of creation destined for destruction. It is the resurrected body of God's creation, evolving through history and brought to its completion with man's co-operation. Father Malevez, S.J. has written: "The present day control over matter, political organizations, art, thought and technology bring Christ to completion and glory." Christians should vie in zeal and generosity to bring this evolution to completion. The only obstacles that hold back the process are those moral evils of selfishness, fear and pride.

Christ, as at the tomb of Lazarus, still stands at the tomb of not only us individually but of the whole world. The whole world is in that tomb, groaning in travail. He is saying continually: "I am the Resurrection and the Life. Come forth, Universe!" But He calls for man's coopera-tion. No activity carried on in this universe, no matter how small and insignificant, will be ever wasted when it is carried on in and through Christ.

Teilhard de Chardin, that modern prophet and mystic, has given the summons to all men to look into this world and see "Jesus Christ shining diaphanously through-out the whole world." He challenges all of us to put away fears and timidity as though we cannot encounter God at the heart of His very matter.

> To adore formerly meant preferring God to things, by referring them back to Him and sacrificing them for Him. To adore now has come to mean pledging oneself body and soul to creative act, by associating oneself with it so as to bring the world to its fulfillment by effort and research. Loving one's neighbor formerly meant not defrauding him and binding up his wounds. Charity, from now on, while not ceasing to be imbued with compassion, will find its fulfillment in a life given for common advance. Being pure formerly meant, in the main, standing aside and preserving oneself from stain. Tomorrow chastity will call, above all, for a sublimation of powers of

flesh and of all passion. Being detached formerly meant not concerning oneself with things and only taking from them the least possible. Being detached now means step-by-step moving beyond all truth and beauty by power of the very love that one bears for them. Being resigned, formerly could signify passive acceptance of present conditions of the universe. . . Being resigned now will no longer be allowed, save to the warrior fainting away in the arms of the angel (*Christologie et Evolution*).

What a dignity is given to man to cooperate with the creative power of God to bring this universe to its fulfillment! By failing to uproot sinfulness in his world, firstly, within his own being, man obstructs the progress of the universe. By seeking to live continually according to the mind of God in all of his relationships, man develops the plan of God.

The early Greek Fathers developed a theology of the dynamic presence of the Logos in all things. St. Maximus the Confessor finds in St. John's Prologue and in the Epistles of St. Paul, especially to the Ephesians and Colossians, the basis for his doctrine of the Logos. Each creature is given a *logos*, a principle of existence which relates it in a dynamic on-going process of creation to God as its cause. God conceived each creature with its proper logos from all eternity, in and through the *LOGOS*, the Second Person of the Trinity in whom and by whom all things were created.

The fully realized Christian is the man who is completely stripped of all sinful attachments so that under the illumination of the Holy Spirit he can contemplate the different *Logoi* in the Logos, Jesus Christ. How much more meaningful would be our love for a human being if we could love him in Jesus Christ! If we could look upon all of God's creatures and see their basic goodness as the mind of God sees them in Christ, how sin and any abuse of God's creation would disappear from our lives and hence somewhat diminish the evil in the world. If people throughout the world could live according to the Logos, they would understand the meaning of a human life and attitudes that now bring about murders, wars, abortions, would change and a better world would result. If married persons could learn to see beyond the superficial level of each other and love each other in Christ, the divorce rate in the world that today is growing to such terrifying proportions and destroying not only the family harmony but also society would diminish radically.

The modern prophet who sees through contemplation the power of Jesus Christ working in the lives of not only Christians but of all human beings, regardless of whatever culture or religion, becomes a citizen of the whole universe. He breaks through the ghetto-concepts of how Jesus Christ should and must work in His universe to see Him in a constant process of evolving through the basic goodness in human beings the universe into its fullness. He begins to see through technology that God is bringing about a cosmic consciousness in the minds of all men throughout the whole world. Distances are shrinking through rapid transportation and instant satellite communications. Above all, psychologically men are living no longer in their own little town or city but are beginning to think as citizens of one gigantic "global village."

Such a prophet points out to the world that "matter is sacred" in the sense of being the point of encounter with a dynamic Trinity that out of love for mankind and a desire to share its divine life with human beings is found inserted "inside" of all created beings. All that has been said in the previous chapters leads up to this vision that the prophet lives by: God's material world has not been conceived by God to be destroyed but to be transfigured and brought into its fullness in and by Jesus Christ.

In a chapel on the campus of Fordham University hangs a bit of modern art called "The Crucifix." It is an assemblage done by an American artist, Albert Ceen, who has taken two pieces of ordinary wood, such as one would find in an orange crate, to form the cross. To this he has attached the "corpus" of the dying Savior, Jesus Christ. But the strange part about this bit of art is that the artist has taken ordinary pieces of junk to fashion the sacred Body of the dying Christ. The halo is a simple stove grate over which a housewife would spend hours cooking meals. The face, distorted in awesome agony, is an ordinary bicycle chain, twisted to form the lineaments of the face of the God-Man in death's struggle. Each arm extended is made up of two monkey wrenches attached to each other. The body is represented in macabre bone-structure outline by an automobile crank case forming the chest down to the legs which are also parts of an automobile motor. The waist and loin cloth are simply a bulky chain wrapt carelessly into a heap.

The spectator's first reaction is one of shock—that the artist should take such junk to depict Christ in the most solemn moment of dying for all men. There is shock also to see the state of total emptiness of Christ on the cross, highlighted by the metallic parts that seem to show only the bare skeleton of a dying man! But after a while the spectator begins to see something else. He begins to enter somewhat into the vision of the artist who wanted to say that the suffering Body of Christ is now being formed by the material elements of this world. A woman in her kitchen, a boy playing with his bicycle, a man driving his truck, the whole material world says a relationship to Jesus Christ. Not only for each person does He die. He seeks also to live in each person and through that person to apply the infinite love of His Father, that sent Him to the cross for love of mankind, to the concrete circumstances in which all human beings live.

It is a vision of a world on march to be transfigured into a Heavenly Jerusalem. The world is far from having reached that goal. Yet the process is moving in a linear progression towards the *Parousia*, the final appearance of Jesus Christ, when He will return in full glory. Then the prophet, who has witnessed to the Transfigured Christ, not only on Mount Tabor, but in his own life of faith and hope during the process of planting, cultivating and pruning, will have the great honor to bring men to the full harvest. He will point to the throne of God and the Lamb.

> And he showed me a pure river of water of life, clear as crystal, proceeding out of the throne of God and of the Lamb. In the midst of the street of it and on either side of the river was there the tree of life, which bore twelve manner of fruits and yielded her fruit every month. And the leaves of the tree were for the healing of the nations.
>
> And there shall be no more curse. But the throne of God and of the Lamb shall be in it and His servants shall serve Him.
>
> And they shall see His face and His name shall be in their foreheads. And there shall be no night there. And they need no candle, neither light of the sun; for the Lord God gives them light and they shall reign forever and ever (Rev. 22:1–5).